The Ultimate Girls' Night In

Also by the author:
Celebrity Style Secrets
The Makeover Book

Jacqui Ripley is a freelance journalist who writes for
Now!, *Cosmopolitan*, *Zest*, *In Style*, the *Evening Standard*
and the *Guardian,* and specialises in health and
beauty. She lives in East London.

The Ultimate Girls' Night In

Jacqui Ripley

PIATKUS

Copyright © 2006 by Jacqui Ripley

First published in 2006 by
Piatkus Books Ltd
5 Windmill Street
London W1T 2JA
Email: info@piatkus.co.uk

Reprinted 2006

The moral right of the author has been asserted
A catalogue record for this book is available from the British Library.

ISBN 0 7499 2697 X

Text design by Goldust Design
Edited by Jan Cutler
Illustrations by Megan Hess

This book has been printed on paper manufactured with respect for the environment using wood from managed sustainable resources.

Printed and bound in Great Britain by
William Clowes Ltd, Beccles, Suffolk

CONTENTS

INTRODUCTION

Staying in – it's the new going out

Where would we be without our girlfriends? They are our sounding board for life, where we download our hopes and fears. So why not celebrate them and throw a girls' night in for your gal pals? Let's face it, girlfriends can be more important than handbags, food and shoes (OK, maybe shoes is going a bit too far!). Perhaps it's because I'm a girl's girl at heart, but I can't think of anything better than throwing a high-style, no-anxiety night in exclusively just for my girlfriends with plenty of fun thrown in. However old you are, eternal girl-hood never loses its appeal, and the thought of a night sprawled out on the sofa, knocking back Manhattans, nibbling on canapés or a takeaway pizza along with indulging in lots of juicy gossip and playing silly games can beat an evening out any time of the week.

The idea of the Ultimate Girls' Night In (UGNI) is to take the pressure off entertaining so that you and your friends can enjoy plenty of fuss-free fun. Whether you decide to invite two or 22 girls round to your place, this book offers something for your special night in. Much like a cocktail recipe, the contents of this book can be shaken about to suit your girls'-night-in style. So, if you fancy slobbing out on the culinary front and speed-dialling in an Indian/Chinese/pizza and spending the night relaxing, then skip Chapter 4 and head for some cool chill-out ideas in Chapter 6. Alternatively, if you want to don a pinny and lay on a bit of bash, then do just that by grabbing some mouth-watering foodie ideas from Chapter 4 and then flipping your way to Chapter 5 for some full-on party games.

The thought of whipping up your little bit of girlie heaven at home is so enticing and this book is crammed full of ideas, recipes and tips to make you and your friends look and feel top-to-toe fabulous. My experience as a beauty editor allows me to bring you tailor-made-to-measure treatments that hit the right (pampering) spot. Within these pages is the know-how you need to turn you into your very own beauty and alternative health guru minus the angst of how much to tip.

If you haven't thought of throwing an UGNI then this book will do all the thinking and planning for you. Stuck for a girlie-night-in theme? Then check out Chapter 1. It's brimming with ideas – from baby showers to hen and movie nights. For the next three chapters it's all about being the best hostess, so if you ever fancied yourself as a cocktail waitress then read on. Otherwise, if you want your night in to be theme-free and you fancy calling in a takeaway, make your way to Chapter 5, which offers suggestions for games to suit any night in, Chapter 6 for those who want to relax including Indian head massage and reflexology, Chapter 7 for ultimate pampering treats including fabulous facials and, finally, Chapter 8, which offers plenty of makeover ideas for make-up, hair and body, which you can easily do with friends. Go right ahead and pick 'n' mix as you please for your best ever (however small or big) night in.

Ah, now doesn't the thought of all of this tempt you to turn your home into a temple of a girl's only delight? Those who aren't up for serious female bonding need not apply.

CHAPTER 1

Preparing your ultimate girls' night in

Throwing a girlie night in doesn't have to have a theme, but a little bit of forward planning never goes amiss and can really help to set the mood. It doesn't matter how many girls you invite round, if the atmosphere isn't there from the beginning the evening can wind up feeling flatter than day-old champagne. Now, it's your night in and you set the rules, but if you're up for throwing a themed night then this chapter has plenty of suggestions. In fact, use this chapter to get you in the Ultimate Girls' Night In (UGNI) mood – even if you don't fancy running with any of the suggested themed ideas, they may well inspire you to come up with your own unique idea suited to your very own night-in style.

Deciding on your night in

OK, where to start? If you're up for setting a themed night in you could start off by being really self indulgent, like throwing a night in because you've bought your most expensive shoes ever and you need to show them off so that your girlfriends can worship them too. Or how about the not-getting-married-yet party? Why should the I'm-so-in-love smug girlfriends have all the fuss and fanfare? If that big-white-dress day seems just too far off for you, why not let your girlfriends sprinkle you with confetti and toast the most important relationship of your life – the one with yourself, of course? Now, I know I'm being silly but, silliness aside, the theme of your party can literally be anything you want. The way to finding your theme is finding clues in the lifestyles of your girlfriends. Is there anyone getting married? Well, that's easy, as a hen night is already in the making. How about a pregnant girlfriend? Then throw her a baby shower (very US, now very everywhere). And what about the wild women of suburbia? Beyond supermarkets and flirting with the guy at the petrol pumps how about a whisky-filled poker night *Desperate Housewives* style? You see, the possibilities are endless and the more girlfriends you think of the more you can become inspired and the more frivolous your theme can be.

Choosing your theme

Now we've established that one way of throwing a get-together is theming your night in, why not use some of these suggestions as a taster to gather the girls? To make your night in really swing (or special), look out for the follow-up ideas for each of the mentioned nights later on in the book.

The Night: Chocolate and Crying, aka The Get-Over-Him Party

In honour of Your dumped girlfriend (she shouldn't be sitting on the sofa with a bottle of wine solo singing 'All By Myself').

7

Evening frolics Picture of said dumper pinned on a dartboard attacked with much sharpened arrows. Guess the Chocolate: the dumpee is blindfolded and squares of different chocolates are put into her mouth. She has to guess what they are. (This is purely medicinal you understand, as chocolate has been revealed to have a lot of amazing chemicals in it, one of which is phenylethylamine – don't bother trying to say it after a few Sea Breezes – that acts as a mild sedative.) Lots of cuddles along with relaxing, pampering and a makeover to make her feel extra loved (see Chapters 6, 7 and 8).

Chick disc 'You Keep Me Hanging On' by Diana Ross and The Supremes.

The Night: Cradles and Cupcakes, aka The Baby Shower

In honour of Your very pregnant girlfriend.

Evening frolics A great pedicure (see Ready-to-wear Feet, Chapter 7). Let's face it, you spend hours looking at your toes during labour so they may as well be buffed and polished. The tipple? Camomile tea for its relaxing qualities. (For great games see Oh Mummy! Games For The Baby Shower, Chapter 5.)

Chick disc 'Make Yours a Happy Home' by Gladys Knight & The Pips.

The Night: Pampering To Go

In honour of I'd-be-a-beauty-therapist-in-my-other-life girlfriends.

Evening frolics Plenty of painting, polishing and preening, along with sloughing, slathering and slicking (check out Super-Easy Massage, Chapter 6; Facing up to Skin Solutions, Chapter 7; and Salon Secrets to Take to Your Bathroom, Chapter 8.)

Chick disc 'You're Beautiful' by James Blunt.

The Night: Chill Out and Relax

In honour of Free-spirited girlfriends.

Evening frolics The chill-out bit includes lots of deep meditative breathing to let out the angst and bring in the calm. (See all of Chapter 6 for great ideas.) And as for the men, this is where your Best Gay Friend (BGF) comes into it (see page 19 for why you should invite him). Boy, does he know the way to a man's inner what-makes-his-mind-tick thinking. If you have no BGF, check out Mystic Hand Signals in Chapter 6 for clues on your man!

Chick disc 'You Make Me Feel Like a Natural Woman' by Carole King.

The Night: Big Date Night

In honour of The girlfriend who thinks he might be The One.

Evening frolics It's the dressing-up scenario to lead him into serious temptation. The shoes that make your legs look up-to-your-armpits long; the bra that belies you're a 32AA; the right colour lipstick that puts a smooch into your pout. (See Chapter 8 for brilliant makeover ideas including the best way to fake a tan – honey-toasted skin is essential for any big date night.)

Chick disc 'Get up (I feel Like Being a) Sex Machine' by James Brown.

The Night: Hen Party, aka The Bachelorette Party

In honour of Your soon-to-be-hitched girlfriend (the one with the big sparkler).

Evening frolics Where do I start? The suggestions are endless (see Games for a Hilarious Hen Night, Chapter 6, for ideas.) A karaoke machine so that you can sing 'I Did Survive', (instead of 'I Will Survive') plus oodles of pampering; having Muriel's Wedding playing constantly in the background.

Chick disc 'Ladies Night' by Kool & The Gang.

The Night: Reality Night

In honour of Your girlfriends who need to feel less dysfunctional.

Evening frolics Mind games – that's what reality TV is all about: picturing the scene of you stranded in the jungle or on an island, or in a house with nine of the least-liked people in your world. How would you handle them? (All of Chapter 6 will help angst-ridden friends chill out and relax with life!)

Chick disc 'Stars of CCTV' by Hard-fi.

The Night: The DVD (I'm-in-the-mood-for-a-movie) Night

In honour of Your movie-buff girlfriends.

Evening frolics Being unashamedly, absolutely, totally girlie in your viewing and lining up: The Doris Day Collection including *Pillow Talk* (surely Rock Hudson wasn't gay?); *Fried Green Tomatoes and The Whistle Stop Café* (the sisterhood at its best); *Grease* (Danny and Sandy rule, OK); any rom-com starring the big-wide-smile herself, Julia Roberts – *Steel Magnolias* would be great to hire and keep an eye on in-between mini makeovers; the film is set around a beauty parlour dontcha know? (See Chapter 8 for fab beauty tips.) *Shrek*. Don't you just love Princess Fiona with that hint of green skin tone? Oh, and let's not forget *Tootsie*. Dustin Hoffman wore some great dresses! (See The

DVD (I'm-in-the-mood-for-a-movie) Night, Chapter 5. And don't forget to check out the movie quiz!)
Chick disc 'Let Me Entertain You' by Robbie Williams.

The Night: Poker and Whisky Night
In honour of The wild, wild women of suburbia. Take inspiration from Sharon Stone in *Casino*.
Evening frolics Mastering a poker face. It's harder than it looks especially after a Cosmopolitan too many. Wising up on poker terms: Bad Beat, Calling Station, Flop, Muck, Rainbow … they do mean something you know, along with knowing your hand rankings: high card, three of a kind and flush. You're then ready to play Blackjack, Hook, Line and Sinker, and Rock 'n' Slots. Check out websites that sell basic poker sets online, including chips, roulette wheels, green felt tables and tip booklets. Now you're ready to hustle girlfriends! (See The Hot-Card Shuffle Poker Night, Chapter 5.)
Chick disc: 'Bad' by Michael Jackson or Vegas mainstays like the Rat Pack.

The Night: Sympathy and Slammers
In honour of The girlfriend having issues with her mother/another girlfriend/boss/mother-in-law-from-hell.
Party frolics After tears and tissues, tea quickly leads to tequila slammers to chase away the blues. (Lighten the

The Poker Cheat Sheet

Post this near the table to remind guests of hand hierarchy. That way no one has to ruin a perfectly good bluff by asking if a pair of ten beats a full house. Smart, hey?

Royal Flush: ace, kings, queen, jack and ten in the same suit

Straight Flush: five cards of the same suit in sequence

Four of a Kind: four cards with the same rank

Full House: three of a kind and a pair

Flush: five cards, any rank in the same suit

Straight: five cards, any suit in sequence

Three of a Kind: three cards with the same rank

Two Pair: two sets of cards of equal rank

High Card: if no one has a pair or better, the highest ranked card wins

mood even further by checking out Frolics for Everyone, Chapter 5.)

Chick disc: 'We Are Family' by Sister Sledge.

The Night: Heels and High Jinks, aka Sex And The City

In honour of The fiendishly fashionable.

Evening frolics Learning the art of walking in red-hot

heels minus the traffic warden stance. Pedicures, naturally. And buffing off callouses caused by desirable but terribly uncomfortable shoes. (This night calls for The Catwalk Caper, Chapter 5, as well as for pampering and preening. Look at Chapters 7 and 8 for suggestions à gogo.)

Chick disc: 'Naughty Girl' by Beyonce.

The Night: Desperate Housewives (for the sometimes not-so-yummy mummies)

In honour of Sick-covered, sleep-deprived mummies.

Evening frolics Laughing hysterically about how you thought you were stressed when you were in a full time job. Remembering the last time you had sex - leisurely. Whipping up an eye mask to disguise the baggage under them. Playing lots of funky dance music to help shift your mood from milky mum to party girl. (Do the Discover Your Dosha quiz in Chapter 6 to find yourself (again!) and Kitchen-Cupboard Beautifying Secrets in Chapter 7, for those chained to the kitchen sink.)

Chick disc 'Relight My Fire' by Dan Hartman (or Take That cover).

The Night: Footballers' Wives

In honour of *The Big Match* lovers.

Evening frolics Singing rowdy football songs, ogling over premier league footballer's thighs and playing along with the footballers' wives bit with a decent manicure and a fake tan (mahogany shade optional). (Beautiful Body Secrets in Chapter 8 ensures you never turn the very fake shade of a wooden door again.)

Chick disc: 'Three Lions (Football's Coming Home)' by the Lightning Seeds with David Baddiel and Frank Skinner.

Bring on the girls (but which ones?)

Your UGNI needs to have the right mix of girlfriends to make it sizzle, crackle and pop. There's no point inviting a hotchpotch of girls who you know don't really get on. The whole point of the evening is to chill – by this I mean be calm, not creating an atmosphere chillier than the Arctic. Remember: when the hostess is relaxed, your guests will be, too. This is where friends' specific plans need to be drawn up. So, for instance, don't invite the recently bitter divorcee to the Hen Night in or the girlfriend who's placed an ad in the lonely-hearts column and hasn't had a single reply to the Big Date Night party. It just doesn't make for one big happy girl fest! But that doesn't mean you can't have an interesting mix of girls – it's just about balance. Here are a handful of girls that we're all familiar with and probably have in our in-crowd; it's just a question of where to slot them.

THE UP-FRONT SINGLETON

She's happy to be unattached, and 'on the shelf' to her means something you pick up from the supermarket. She pities Bridget Jones ('That woman is just so tragic. Who can be that desperate for a man? She needs to get a life.') This singleton is perfect for Heels and High Jinks. She can also quite easily be slotted into Chill Out and Relax night in as she has good karma about her where it concerns men.

THE OUTRAGEOUS GOSSIP

This girl can talk for England. Make that Ireland and Wales, too. She works in public relations and knows everybody and everything. Outside of the gossip papers she's in the know about who's sleeping with whom, who will be bedding whom and who's checked into rehab. This gossiper is perfect for the Desperate Housewives night. Those mummies need an injection of gossip running through their veins to remind them there's more to the daily nappy/poo/lack-of-sleep gossip outside mummy world.

THE THERAPY (NUT) CASE

A great friend but with even greater issues. She uses therapy as an emotional crutch and spends most of her week visiting her colour therapist searching for her aura, her acupuncturist searching for her meridians, her aromatherapist to soothe away her stress, her reflexologist to find and treat her inner angst and, of course, her shrink (poor guy) to sort out her muddled head. A great guest for the Chill Out and Relax night (deep breathing is second nature to her), also the Reality Night. All those mad people actually make her look sane.

THE BABY MAKER

This girl can't stop popping them out. She is in baby heaven and she can't stop gurgling about them. This can be boring once she gets on a roll (she can recite the whole contents list of the Mothercare catalogue) but she's the poster girl for the ultimate Baby Shower. Her role will be 'mothering' the mum-ready-to-drop and will advise and comfort away her fears – of which there will be many. The DVD night is just her thing, too. Those baby-making hormones constantly circulating around her body make her ideal for those weepy movies.

What makes a good girlfriend?

- She keeps your very dark secrets to herself.
- She doesn't judge or try to change you.
- She makes you laugh until you cry.

What makes A bad girlfriend?

- She constantly criticises you.
- She asks if you've lost weight yet.
- She's always last at the bar and first out the taxi (meaning she never pays her way).

THE DIVA

This girlfriend is Marilyn Monroe, Liza Minnelli and Mariah Carey all rolled into one. She's had tragedy (does a broken nail count?), she's glamorous and, boy, is she demanding! She arrives always enveloped in a cloud of Chanel No. 5 or a bespoke fragrance a sugar daddy has created for her. Heels and High Jinks is very much her party, as is Poker and Whisky. Oh, and she gives great sex tips, too. Where she picks them up from you daren't ask!

THE BEAUTY JUNKIE

Her hobby is staking out the beauty floor of a department store and, just like the Therapy Case, she relies on an arsenal of experts to get her through the week. Although hers are Gino her Italian hairdresser, Frieda her colourist, Maisy her masseur and Iris her manicurist and pedicurist. Her knowledge in the pampering area is phenomenal. Of course, the Pampering To Go party has her name written all over it. She'd love the Footballers' Wives party also; she's always appreciative of a man with a waxed torso.

BEST GAY FRIEND (BGF)

He's been mentioned earlier, but I'll mention him again, because he can be key for an unforgettable night. Apart from knowing the inner workings of the alpha male (great for the Hen Night in) he has a superb eye for fashion – so perfect for the Big Date Night party and is also great for smoothing over a crisis. What he doesn't know about handling a tetchy mother-in-law can be written on a napkin. A Sympathy and Slammers night in would be the party to invite him to.

THE DRAMA QUEEN

Making mountains out of molehills and brewing up a storm in a teacup is what this girl is all about. She literally stars in her own life (in the leading role of course) moving through her day as if she's auditioning for Scarlett O'Hara – and you love her for it, as life is never dull when she is around. Book her in for the Reality Night.

PARTY POOPER Drinking out of plastic cups. It just doesn't set the tone for a high-class evening. Hire glasses if need be.

PARTY SOOTHER Make each girlfriend feel special by greeting her with a flourish of kisses and magically appearing with a cocktail.

CHAPTER 2

The hostess with the mostest

If throwing and hosting a night in brings you out in hives and puts you into a spin – then relax, it's easy. Honest. What you've got to remember is that you're entertaining your girlfriends, not the Royals, so the pressure is off to turn into the Domestic Goddess. Remember, it's your call how you want to host your

UGNI. If all you want is a low key night where you gather a handful of friends for a gossip, then fancy invites, cute canapés and a cocktail shaker may not be necessary – hey, a bottle of Pinot Grigio, a few munchies, the promise of a manicure and an all-time favourite movie is the only temptation your close friends need! But, saying that, if you want to push the party boat out then this chapter is for you, as it reveals the hottest hosting tips and helps turn you into one hip party planner. Here are some ideas for simple invites and fuss-free but cheery decor. Remember: inviting friends into your home is, and should be, fun.

How to plan your night in

Get yourself organised so that your night in feels special and is not the same as when your friends just pop round for an impromptu visit.

DATE AND TIME

If a theme has been chosen, to a certain extent you can base many of your decisions about the food, drinks, decorations and times around it. For example a Friday night might not be an ideal slot for a Baby Shower party: the mum-to-be could be ready to hit the sack before she's even out the door. A Saturday night may be better, as she's had the whole day to feel more relaxed. And holding a Poker and Whisky get-together on a Sunday night would be lethal if you have to roll into work on Monday. For that one earmark a Friday night and then even if it goes on into the early hours of Saturday morning you'll have all day Sunday to recover (and clear up).

INVITATIONS

These set the mood for the party. Ideally send them out a week before, as this gives people the time to reserve the date. However, sometimes spontaneity in a party is crucial, as it feels wonderfully frivolous. So, if your social life is flatlining and you have the urge to shake up a few cocktails and the craving for a good belly laugh, then e-mail a few invites that afternoon with the invitation to hang out at your place the next evening.

This leads me nicely into invitations. The beauty of e-mail is that you can send invites fast and furious – it's much cheaper and you can be assured that everyone gets their invite, but it also signals a very informal do. In other words you can never be too sure if friends will turn up, or, equally, that your email will be circulated to anyone and everyone. If you don't want your party to become an open house, try to make it clear on the invite that it's for close girlfriends only. There's nothing worse than having your invite forwarded to dozens of 'address books'! Posting an invite, however, will mean guests will make more effort to RSVP and treat it is an occasion.

Cool invites
Simply jot (or tie) information about your party onto:
- A suspender belt for the Hen Party
- A dummy for the Baby Shower
- A condom for the Big Date Night party
- An ace card for the Poker and Whisky party
- A packet of tissues for Chocolate and Crying.

Dress code
Not a lot to say here, but just because you're staying at home doesn't mean you can pad around in stained tops and baggy pants. At least wear a clean T-shirt and baggy pants! Otherwise, slip on your frock and sparkle. Tuxedo shirts for Poker and Whisky are optional! For the Pampering To Go Party ask everybody to bring their bathrobes – they're a great leveller at the beginning of the night in, and, once pampered, guests can then make-up and dress up if they want.

PARTY POOPER Throwing a party just after New Year's Eve. Everybody is detoxing.

PARTY SOOTHER Having parties off-season. Everyone needs to glam up during the cold winter months.

Setting the scene

If the place looks tidy and you have given a little thought to the ambience of the room, your night in is more likely to start off well.

ULTRA-QUICK CLEAN-UP

You are expecting guests so it's only polite to clean up. But hold the Mrs Mop get-up, as an emergency clean up doesn't have to be a back-breaking chore; a little flick with the duster combined with dim lighting will give the illusion of turning your pad into a palace.

• **Open all windows** before you start dust busting. Not only will it air the room but there is nothing that quashes an atmosphere faster than the smell of furniture polish.

- **Change the sheets** on your bed. A girlfriend may feel a little unwell after too much bubbly and need to lie down. Lying in toast crumbs won't make her feel better.
- **Wipe all surfaces** with a slightly damp cloth to get rid of dust.
- **Clean your bathroom.** Hoover up stray hairs on the floor, in the washbasin and remove from the soap (yuk!). Even better, put out a fresh new bar. Remove any clutter such as combs, manky razors, used pore strips (they're for your fascination only) and clogged up shampoo bottles. Bring out the clean towels.
- **In the kitchen** wash up any dirty crockery. You don't want your place looking like student digs. Again, clear any clutter from the surfaces.
- **Have you a treasured coffee table?** Then put out coasters for drinks. Likewise, if you have a favourite rug and don't want a Cosmopolitan or any other coloured drink spilt on it, roll it up and put it away.
- **Leave enough floor space** for guests to mix and mingle.
- **Leave out celebrity magazines** like *Hello!* Girls love dissecting the rich and famous for flaws.
- **When it comes to smokers**, if you'd rather they smoke outside then put ashtrays out in the garden. But let's face it, if you're throwing a night

in then house rules should be relaxed. Don't treat smokers as unwanted vermin!

- **Guests may misplace their drinks** so plenty of glassware is key. If there isn't enough in your cupboard, beg, borrow or buy.
- **Fill your freezer with ice** for drinks. Also, consider ordering ice through a delivery service. It's less hassle and is cheaper than you think.

Multi-task while cleaning

(also known as taking the horror out of housework)

We all know housework is dull, dull, dull, so why not liven it up a little by bribing yourself with little treats to get your inner dust buster working?

- Put on a deep hair-conditioning mask or face mask. They can 'cook' while you're vacuuming.
- Use the housework as exercise. Your body doesn't know the difference between working out in the gym or pushing a Hoover.
- If your boyfriend is around, do the housework in your best undies. The reward will be waiting for you afterwards!
- Play great tunes and turn the volume up loud. Very loud.
- Promise yourself a big bubble bath at the end of cleaning. Just don't forget to clean out the tub afterwards!

THE BIG CLEAR UP

OK, we've had the clean up and now it's time for the clear up. It doesn't have to be a drama. Although this section feels that it should be in the last chapter, after all, the party has well and truly ended then, there are some points in it that need to be read now – while sober and before bed – if you want to keep your home looking and smelling sweet. If it's late (and it will be) don't try to do all the cleaning straight away before going to bed. Simply deal with anything smelly such as emptying ashtrays and throwing away leftover food and paper plates. Tip out the last dregs of cocktails from glasses and group them together in one area.

- Open a window, if only for five minutes, to freshen the room.
- Blow out candles before hitting your pillow.
- Next day, turn up the music – hangover permitting – and tackle each task: washing glasses, vacuuming and taking out rubbish. Afterwards, head to the pub for a hair-of-the-dog.

Damage limitation

- **Stains** Treat asap after you notice them. Soak with a little mineral water to help draw out the stain and then tackle it in the morning.
- **Candle wax on carpets** Rub ice cubes over the patch to harden the wax and then scrape off as much as possible. Place paper towels over the remaining wax and press with a cool iron to lift the rest of it away.
- **Water marks on any surface** Use a small amount of toothpaste and rub in. Leave for a few minutes before removing with a damp, clean cloth.
- **Cigarette burns on carpets** Snip away the singed edges with manicure scissors and use tweezers to remove burned fibres. If all else fails buy a rug!

Encourage at-home lounging

Create an intimate vibe and make your home feel welcoming by dimming the lights and plumping up the cushions on the sofa to create a relaxing atmosphere.

FLOWERS

I don't want to come over all Martha Stewart here, and I'm not suggesting you hit the flower markets at the crack of dawn to nab all the best blooms, but flowers are a lovely detail to have in a room and can save you money on room spray, too! Back off from the fancy arrangements though; all you need are a few vases of the same flower. Include daisies, sunflowers, lilies and irises, which are classed as the happiest and girliest flowers you can find.

The music

A fab party starts with the playlist. I like to call it 'funkology', as the right groove for your party is essential. It will immediately help to create a great atmosphere. Get it right and your party will rock, get it wrong and it can kill it. I'm still recovering from a dinner party I went to years ago where The Clash was played all night! Hanging out in a club, great. Sitting down to a meal of fish and wine, not so great. You don't have to be up and down all night choosing discs either, use an iPod – it's an ideal DIY DJ tool. Simply programme in your favourite tracks, connect it to your stereo and hide away your precious CDs (why is it that girlfriends always seem to borrow them but never seem to return them?).

THE EFFORTLESS HOME-MADE TOUCH

Think about comfort, relaxation and something a little special.

The lighting

The general rule is: dim down to lighten up. During the day you want as much light as possible to flood a room, but after 6.00 p.m. you want to take the wattage down a notch or two. Soft lighting and candles not only put those chocolate and wine stains on the sofa into hiding (from too many Bridget Jones evenings) but also give a relaxed ambiance to the room and, more importantly, make everybody look prettier and younger: good lighting equals a fabulous complexion! And what girl doesn't want that? For low-level lighting either trade normal light bulbs for peachy soft ones, switch on table lamps to improve the atmosphere, or litter the room with pretty fairy lights draped over picture frames, mirrors, mantelpieces or bundled into glass bowls. Or use candles. But a cautionary word: as the saying goes there's no smoke without fire, so ensure all tea lights are in fireproof holders – a drunken fling of the arm can send a candle flying and leave a nasty burnt hole in the carpet. As for burning a scented candle all night, the fragrance can wind up becoming a little overwhelming after a while and leave the room smelling like that of a perfume hall and guests a tad queasy. Light it for an hour or so before the girls arrive then blow it out. It will leave the room with just the right delicate aroma.

Cushions

What self-respecting girl doesn't have a cushion wardrobe she can call on in times of crisis? You know only too well that an oversized plumped-up cushion helps soften the blow of a pull-your-hair-out day. So scatter them around generously on sofas and toss on the floor to create a cosy lounging area. Talking about comfort, for your DVD or Reality Night parties arrange your seating around a low coffee table facing your TV. Make sure each seat is near a flat surface on which to place food and drinks and, of course, a clear view of the television.

Party bags

You may think party bags went out of fashion after you were five years old – not so. When I went over to a friend's to celebrate her birthday recently she sent everybody away with a party bag. And do you know what? It was a perfect ending to a fun-filled evening, as every girlfriend felt special. I think it's nice to give mini bags that reflect the theme of the party, so, for example, why not put a few luxury Belgian chocolates into a bag for the Chocolate and Crying night, satin eye masks for the Pampering To Go party or little thought cards (buy as a pack and split up) into the Chill Out and Relax evening bags.

What makes a perfect guest?

There's been much talk about being the hostess with the mostest but what about being a brilliant guest? Here are a few pointers on girls' night-in etiquette:

- Don't expect to be waited on all night. Help yourself to drinks and food, and offer to get some for other guests, too.
- Help without being asked. Clear and stack the dishes, for example, when everybody has stopped nibbling.
- Don't harp on about any special dietary measures you may have. Simply eat or don't.
- Don't be too overenthusiastic. If your hostess says she doesn't need help then believe her. There's nothing more annoying than a busybody hovering in the background!
- Bring something to the party – wine, mixers or a favourite CD.
- Don't monopolise the conversation.

PARTY POOPER Don't stress about your guest list. People will cancel last minute and there are those who will ask if they can bring someone you don't know. Just go with the flow. Give a big hello and welcome her – you never know what the mystery girl can bring to the mix.

PARTY SOOTHER Invite your closest girlfriend to come around an hour before everybody else arrives. Crack open a bottle of bubbly together to get you in the mood to party.

CHAPTER 3
The drinks

When planning and plotting a girlie night, a pint of lager and a packet of crisps sometimes doesn't cut the mustard. A girls' night in calls for nothing less than cocktails and other fancy drinks. So think cool. Think fruity. Think refreshing. Cocktails are fashionable, thanks, in part to Carrie and co. in *Sex and the City*. And for the ultra-busy (and glamorous) hostess, cock-tails are a great way to entertain any kind of guest, whether it's your high-kicking or baby-in-the-womb-kicking girlfriend – although her cocktail would be a virgin one naturally!

And, if you really want to feel good about shaking them up you can even kid yourself that they are (almost) a healthy tonic in a glass. Yes, your inner nutritionist will tell you that if you go overboard on the fruit then arguably your cocktail can count towards your five portions of fruit and vegetable intake a day. The fresher the fruit joices in your cocktail the better, as they will harbour more good-for-you content.

THE LOW-FUSS COCKTAIL RULES

The thought of serving cocktails continuously for a night in can exhaust a hostess before she's even sent the invites out, as many people wrongly assume that it must involve a lot of time, effort and expense. First off, you cannot be expected to lay out for a whole bar full of spirits, so have a chat with your girlfriends about the cocktail menu. The rule here is to limit the number to about two or three and then make a decision about who's bringing which bottle. It would be unreasonable and un-sisterly to look to the hostess to supply all the drink herself, unless of course you'd won the lottery or you are going out with the owner of a bar. The bill will

Serving fab-tini cocktails

Let's start with the basics. You will need:

- **Shaker** Use it to blend and chill mixed drinks.
- **Glasses** Already mentioned (no to plastic cups or, worse, mugs). Have martini glasses for chilled drinks and lowball glasses for anything splashed on the rocks – or even wine. Champagne flutes are a nice touch, too, for anything drunk, well, with champagne!
- **Ice buckets** if you want to be chic. A classy hostess has a small bowl or bucket for the rocks plus a scoop or spoon for serving.
- **Jigger** A one-and-half measure takes the guesswork out of cocktail prepping and may save you from a major hangover. Measures poured at home are a lot more generous than at a bar.
- **Kitsch trays** A tray makes the cocktails look exciting and special. Have two: one to offer fresh cocktails, the other to take away the empties.
- **Decorations** Cute little neon straws, mini Chinese-style umbrellas, swizzle sticks and fresh fruit make cocktails look like they have been poured down from girlie heaven.

be large and you'll be resentful about it before you've even begun to shake the first cocktail. But make it clear that you will supply mixers, decorations and ice along with coffee and tea to nurse fragile heads later in the evening. So that everybody can get in on the shake-it-and-mix-it act, ask friends to bring over extra cocktail shakers and blenders otherwise you'll be stuck in the kitchen all night whizzing up drinks.

WHAT MIXERS DO I NEED?

Leaving aside the alcohol content for a moment or two, there are other crucial elements to the well-stocked cocktail bar. Depending on the cocktails you're planning to serve you may need any or all of the following ingredients:

- **Juices** That's orange, cranberry, grapefruit, tomato, pineapple, lemon or lime juice. Freshly squeezed where possible for a tastier drink. For freshly squeezed juices you can estimate that the average lemon or lime will give you about 30 ml/1 fl oz/ 2 tablespoons of juice, an orange between 40–85 ml/1¼–3 fl oz of juice depending on its size.
- **Carbonated drinks** Club soda, tonic water, lemonade, ginger ale.
- **Flavouring ingredients** These give a kick to the

cocktails: salt, pepper, horseradish, sugar, grena-dine, simple syrup, coconut cream.

- **Funky ingredients** Keep your cocktails hip by keeping up on the latest cocktail trends. The current hot mixer for vodka, for example, is an energy drink. Research what's current at your favourite cocktail hangout or on the net and have some on hand.
- **Salt and sugar (again)** If you're planning on rimming cocktail glasses for the professional touch.
- **Milk, cream and whipped cream**, or possibly even ice cream.
- **Decorations** Lemon or lime peel or wedges, cherries, olives, cocktail onions or celery sticks.

THE TEN ULTIMATE CLASSIC COCKTAILS

Mention cocktails and everybody will have their favourite, but unless you've been a cocktail shaker in a previous life, getting to grips with a huge variety of cocktails will leave you shaken and feeling very stirred! The trick is to stick to the classics where you can be confident that everyone is likely to find something they will enjoy from the drinks menu. If anyone of your girlfriends wants something a little more kitsch or kooky encourage her to bring the spirits and make her trendy tipples herself.

It's cocktail o' clock!
Drink with a great big smile. Each recipe serves one.

MANHATTAN
Created by a bartender who worked at the Manhattan Club, New York in 1874. Sir Winston Churchill's mother threw a party and requested a new drink. This was it.

You will need
37.5 ml/1¼ fl oz/2½ tablespoons whisky or bourbon
7.5 ml/¾ fl oz/1½ teaspoons sweet vermouth
dash of bitters
maraschino cherry with a stem, to decorate

Sip it real good
Pour the ingredients over ice into a shaker and shake for at least 30 seconds. Decorate with a maraschino cherry with a stem.

COSMOPOLITAN
Origins unknown but has recently had a renaissance thanks to its reputation as a liquid staple for the *Sex and the City* Girls.

You will need
45 ml/1¹/₂ fl oz/3 tablespoons vodka
20 ml/³/₄ fl oz/4 teaspoons Cointreau
7.5 ml/¹/₄ fl oz/1¹/₂ teaspoons lime juice
20 ml/³/₄ fl oz/4 teaspoons cranberry juice
lemon wedge, lemon twist or orange peel, to decorate

Sip it real good
Shake all the ingredients with ice and strain into a martini glass. Decorate with a lemon wedge, lemon twist or orange peel.

BLOODY MARY
Hails from Harry's New York Bar in Paris in the roaring 1920s. Take a cocktail note that: Tequila makes it a Bloody Maria, Gin makes it a Red Snapper, minus the vodka a Virgin Mary or a Bloody Shame!

You will need
50 ml/2 fl oz/¹/₄ cup vodka
90 ml/3 fl oz/6 tablespoons tomato juice
15 ml/¹/₂ fl oz/1 tablespoons lemon juice
salt and ground black pepper
3 dashes of Worcestershire sauce
2 drops of Tabasco sauce
celery stick, to decorate

Sip it real good
Stir all ingredients into a highball glass with ice. Finish off with a celery stick.

BELLINI
Invented at Harry's Bar in Venice. It was named after the artist Giovanni Bellini (c. 1430–1516).

You will need
30 ml/1 fl oz/2 tablespoons fresh peach purée or nectar
90 ml/3 fl oz/6 tablespoons chilled champagne
fresh peach slice, to decorate

Sip it real good
Put the peach purée or nectar in a champagne flute and fill with chilled champagne. Decorate with a fresh peach slice.

PINA COLADA

This tropical girlie tipple was actually first shaken up in Barcelona rather than the Caribbean. It's name comes from the Spanish phrase for strained pineapple!

You will need

50 ml/2 fl oz/¼ cup light rum
150 ml/5 fl oz/¼ pint pineapple juice
50 ml/2 fl oz/¼ cup coconut cream
1 cup of crushed ice
fresh cherries and pineapple, to decorate

Sip it real good

Pour all the ingredients into a blender and whizz at high speed. Pour into a Collins (short) glass and decorate with fresh cherries and pineapple. For that Caribbean vibe, stick in plenty of umbrellas. Firework optional!

SEA BREEZE

The original of the Breeze cocktails. Why not also try a Bay Breeze with pineapple or a Caribbean Breeze with coconut rum?

You will need
50 ml/2 fl oz/¹/₄ cup vodka
90 ml/3 fl oz/6 tablespoons cranberry juice
50 ml/2 fl oz/¹/₄ cup grapefruit juice
lime wedge, to decorate

Sip it real good
Pour all the ingredients into a shaker and shake with ice. Strain into a highball (tall) glass and decorate with a lime wedge.

MARGARITA

The most popular story to explain the origins of this cocktail is that a fabulous hostess and socialite, Margarita Sames, hosted a party where the party game of choice was to make up cocktails. Her guests loved hers so much the recipe soon became a favourite with the Hollywood elite.

You will need
45 ml/1¹/₂ fl oz/3 tablespoons tequila
15 ml/¹/₂ fl oz/1 tablespoon Cointreau
30 ml/1 fl oz/2 tablespoons lime juice
lime juice, salt and a slice of lime, to decorate

Sip it real good

Rub the rim of a chilled Margarita glass with lime and dip into salt to coat it. In a cocktail shaker, mix the ingredients with ice. Shake and strain into the glass. Decorate with a slice of lime.

TOM COLLINS

So popular this cocktail has a glass named after it. There are many stories circulating about this drink, but my favourite is that an Irish immigrant, Tom Collins, who worked as a bartender in New Jersey, New York, tried to beat the heat by making this drink to sip without 'getting tight'. Friends tried it, liked it and it became his signature drink.

You will need

37.5 ml/1¼ fl oz/2½ tablespoons gin
sour mix
splash of soda
orange slice or cherry, to decorate

Sip it real good

Shake the gin and sour mix with ice. Pour into a Collins glass, top with soda and decorate with an orange slice or cherry.

DIRTY MARTINI

This cocktail made its spirited appearance in the 1930s: the end of prohibition was toasted with a Dirty Martini. Traditionally a Martini is made with gin, but if vodka is used it becomes dirty! Vermouth is an option in this recipe.

You will need

45 ml/1½ fl oz/3 tablespoons gin or vodka
15 ml/½ fl oz/1 tablespoon dry vermouth (optional)
30 ml/1 fl oz/2 tablespoons olive juice
2 olives

Sip it really good

Place an ice cube and a small amount of water (15 ml/½ fl oz/ 1 tablespoon) in a cocktail glass and pop in the fridge until chilled. Fill a mixer with all the ingredients. Shake hard three to four times. Strain the contents into the chilled cocktail glass.

BETWEEN THE SHEETS

Hell, who knows the history of this one? All you need to know is it's potent and has a name to rival that of Sex on the Beach. A great toast for a hen night.

You will need

20 ml/¾ fl oz/4 teaspoons rum
20 ml/¾ fl oz/4 teaspoons brandy
20 ml/¾ fl oz/4 teaspoons Cointreau
splash of fresh lemon juice
slice of lime and a cherry, to decorate

Sip it real good
Combine all the ingredients in a shaker over ice. Strain into a chilled glass. Serve with a slice of lime and a cherry.

Drinking games

There's never a better excuse to play games than when tipsy (more of which later in Chapter 5), but here are two drinking games you can start off with:

Kings Shuffle one deck of cards. Start dealing one card at a time, face up, to each player. The first person to be dealt a king picks a liquor, the second person dealt a king picks the mixer, the third dealt a king makes the drink and the last dealt a king drinks it.

Drink or Dare Everyone is familiar with the game Truth or Dare and everyone knows the Truth half is usually lame! The whole point is to dare others to do ridiculous stuff. Therefore, replace the 'Truth' option with 'Drink'. When electing not to take a dare, the victim instead downs a drink. In no time, everyone is feeling tipsy and ready for some absurd dares.

SEASONAL COCKTAILS

As Miss Cocktail it's sometimes fun to offer a cocktail of the season. The best bars in town do, so why not at your pad?

Spring
The weather's warming up, so it's time to start looking forward to summer.

HONEY GIRL
You will need

37.5 ml/¼ fl oz/2½ tablespoons Cachara
15 ml/½ fl oz/1 tablespoons coconut cream
15 ml/½ fl oz/1 tablespoon cream
30 ml/1 fl oz/2 tablespoons pineapple juice
2 teaspoons honey
a slice of pineapple, to decorate

Sip it real good
Fill a fancy glass with crushed ice. Mix all the ingredients except the honey with ice cubes in a shaker and strain into the glass. Add the honey and decorate by adding a slice of pineapple onto the side of the glass.

Summer

Cool off with something refreshing.

MINT JULEP
You will need

¹/₂ teaspoon sugar
12 fresh mint leaves
20 ml/³/₄ fl oz/4 teaspoons water
50 ml/2 fl oz/¹/₄ cup bourbon
mint leaves, to decorate

Sip it real good

In the bottom of a chilled highball glass mix the sugar, mint leaves and water until the sugar is dissolved. Add crushed ice then pour over the bourbon. Decorate with mint.

Autumn

Warmer drinks for when evenings are getting colder.

CEDARWOOD
You will need

30 ml/1 fl oz/2 tablespoons lemon juice
50 ml/2 fl oz/¹/₄ cup vodka
125 ml/4 fl oz/¹/₂ cup cranberry juice
90 ml/3 fl oz/6 tablespoons ginger ale

Sip it real good
In a tall glass over ice combine the lemon juice, vodka, cranberry juice and ginger ale. Stir and serve.

Winter
Get festive.

THE MISTLETOE
You will need
1 sugar cube
15 ml/¹/₂ fl oz/1 tablespoon apple brandy
15 ml/¹/₂ fl oz/1 tablespoon cranberry juice
125 ml/4 fl oz/¹/₂ cup champagne
apple slice, to decorate

Sip it real good
Drop a sugar cube into a champagne flute. Add the apple brandy and the cranberry juice. Slowly add the champagne (it will foam up) and stir gently, trying not to break the sugar cube. Set an apple slice on the inner rim of the flute.

DRINK WITH A PUNCH

A well-mixed punch with plenty of kick in it makes for a fab ice-breaker at a party. It's great to greet the girls with a glass of punch that's already been made, saving you nipping off to the kitchen every time the doorbell rings to whisk up a cocktail. Adjust measures to how many girls you've got coming round. Try these two easy recipes. Each recipe serves about 20 (two or three glasses each).

BOMBAY PUNCH
You will need
1 litre/1³/₄ pints brandy
1 litre/1³/₄ pints sherry
125 ml/4 fl oz/¹/₂ cup maraschino liqueur
300 ml/10 fl oz/¹/₂ pint orange curaçao
200 m/8 fl oz Club Soda
4 bottles of champagne (you can cheat with cava)
fresh fruit, to decorate

Sip it real good
Place your punch bowl into a larger bowl that is already filled with ice. Mix all the ingredients together and decorate with plenty of fresh fruit, tropical style.

HAPPY HOUR PUNCH
You will need
1 litre/1³/₄ pints Southern Comfort
300 ml/10 fl oz/¹/₂ pint pineapple juice
300 ml/10 fl oz/¹/₂ pint grapefruit juice
150 ml/5 fl oz/¹/₄ pint lemon juice
4 bottles of champagne (or cava)
orange slices, to decorate

Sip it real good

Mix all the ingredients together except the champagne. Add the bubbly and ice just before serving. Decorate with orange slices.

PARTY POOPER Trying not to become a self-pitying party girl after one drink far too many. It's never a good idea to be drunk and dialling, or indeed, tipsy and texting your ex when fuelled with potent cocktails.

PARTY SOOTHER Having just enough drink to loosen your tongue for sparkly, witty and funny conversation along with 'No!, you didn't!' anecdotes.

Make mine a mocktail

In your role as a spirited mixologist be aware that not everybody may want to drink much alcohol – especially at the baby shower. Have a few non-alcoholic cocktail recipes up your sleeve that look just as good served alongside the real ones. Here are a few to whet a teetotaller's thirst:

I'LL FAKE MANHATTAN
You will need
45 ml/1¹/₂ fl oz/3 tablespoons each of cranberry and orange juice
2 dashes of orange bitters
dash of grenadine and lemon juice

Sip it real good
Stir all the ingredients over ice and serve up in a chilled cocktail glass.

CINDERELLA
You will need
50 ml/2 fl oz/¹/₄ cup orange juice
50 ml/2 fl oz/¹/₄ cup pineapple juice
splash of sour mix
dash of grenadine
splash of soda
maraschino cherry, to decorate

Sip it real good
Shake all the ingredients except the soda over ice. Strain over fresh ice in a Collins glass. Top with soda. Decorate with a maraschino cherry.

BEACH BLANKET BINGO

You will need

90 ml/3 fl oz/6 tablespoons cranberry juice
90 ml/3 fl oz/6 tablespoons grapefruit juice
90 ml/3 fl oz/6 tablespoons club soda
lime wedge, to decorate

Sip it real good

Build the juices over ice in a Collins glass. Top with soda.
Decorate with a lime wedge.

The how-to list on handling your hangover

You know before you've even had your first sip of punch or got your lips around the rim of a cocktail glass that you might be suffering big time tomorrow with the hangover from hell. But it's a small price to pay for the UGNI - isn't it? Well, yes maybe it is, but why not get hangover smart? Apart from ordering in a lorry load of aspirin, wise up on some of the alternative remedies and cures you can take for the morning after the night before. Put them into action as soon as that headache comes a knocking from too much girlie spirit.

THE YOGA CURE

Believe it or not yoga can be great for a hangover. The key is to avoid forceful forward or backward bending, which changes the pressure in your head. For relief try neck rolling. Face forward and take a deep breath. Breathing out, bend your head gently forward until your chin is pressed into your chest. Move your head slowly and gently in a circular motion from the left until your head tilts slightly backward. Continue to roll your head in the same direction until your chin is pressed into your chest again. You should feel a gentle stretch in your neck, which will help release tension in your head.

THE AROMATHERAPY CURE

Run a warm aromatic bath by adding two drops of fennel (calming), two drops of juniper (detoxifying) and two drops of rosemary (stimulating) essential oils. In the meantime add one drop of peppermint oil and one drop of rose oil into warm honey water, and drink.

THE DETOX CURE

Look to this Liver Recovery cocktail: use a juicer to juice two apples, six strawberries and a banana. Blend with a handful of ice cubes and pour over the rocks.

THE REFLEXOLOGY CURE

Massaging the foot will generally help balance the body, improve circulation, restore mental alertness and enhance nerve function. But specifically applying pressure through the pad of your big toe will increase blood flow to your brain and help ease the pain of a hangover. Use your thumb to creep along your big toe as if it were a caterpillar (small movements) while resting your foot sideways on your knee.

THE HERBAL CURE

Take milk thistle, otherwise known as the prickly protector. Taken either as a supplement or a tincture, it supports the liver, encouraging the cells to reproduce and regenerate. It also helps metabolise alcohol. Take an hour before you go out, when you're out and before you go to bed.

THE HOMEOPATHIC CURE

A fragile head, nausea and irritability will be encouraged to move on with the homeopathic remedy Nux vomica (Nux-v.). For a stonking hangover take 30c every 15 minutes for three doses, then as required. It's advised not to take peppermint or drink coffee when taking homeopathic medicine or it simply won't work.

THE HOLISTIC CURE

Meditate to alleviate! Lie down in a dimly lit room and count four breaths in, hold for four and then breathe out for four. In your mind's eye visualise a strong healthy heart pumping blood around the body and picture your alcohol-abused liver cleansed and strong. However, if there's no time to meditate, handle your hangover on the go by pinching and pulling your ears to stimulate awareness and concentration.

THE PERSONAL-FITNESS CURE

Cells need oxygen and water to function, so take a bottle of water and go for a brisk half-hour walk. It clears the head and does wonders for the constitution. Honest!

THE NUTRITIONIST'S CURE

Hangover-proof yourself before you go. Don't drink on an empty stomach. The presence of food in the stomach helps decrease the concentration of alcohol by diluting it. Food also helps delay the absorption of alcohol. Nibble throughout your drinking escapade along with drinking water in between your cocktails. By starting out with food and replenishing your body as you drink, you reduce your chances of a hangover.

THE VITAMIN CURE

Take vitamin B complex before going out and before bed. This should help process the alcohol.

THE SPA THERAPIST CURE

Make a cup of tea and then pop the tea bags over your eyes. This will reduce puffiness and help to calm bloodshot eyes. Next, rid headaches, blocked sinuses and an all-over ache by running a hot bath and adding some Vicks VapoRub. It will help release muscular aches and pains.

THE AURVEYDIC CURE

Drink coconut water (present in young coconuts and from health food stores). The sweetness increases energy and promotes good digestion.

THE NURTURING CURE

Hydrate. Drink as much mineral water as possible. You body needs fluids to break down the alcohol. Secondly, you can't beat a strong cup of black coffee with a little sugar to help raise lowered glucose levels depleted by alcohol, kick-start the system and wake up the brain.

Lastly, what better excuse to eat a fry up of bacon and eggs – all that protein can really help mop up the after effects of alcohol.

THE COCKTAIL TEA

Try this stomach-soothing ginger and mint tea. Infuse 4 tablespoons chopped lemongrass, 5 tablespoons thinly sliced fresh root ginger (with skin) and two or three mint leaves in six cupfuls of hot water. Drink with a teaspoon of honey added.

THE PARTY-GIRL CURE

Stay in bed and sleep it off!

How to look like you've slept when you haven't

It's one thing feeling like a dog's dinner, but another to look like one. Baggy eyes, a bloated face and greasy hair do not make for a good look. Here are some quick-fix tips to bluff the fact that you've only slept for three hours instead of eight.

- Never use concealer 'neat' under the eye area in the hope of disguising lines and bags. The dryness and thickness alone will make skin look older and tired. Simply mix with a little eye cream and then pat on with your ring finger.
- Leave two teaspoons in the fridge overnight. In the morning press them against your puffy eyes and see what a difference it makes.
- Curl your lashes. This small step has the biggest effect on waking up a tired face.
- Moisturise aplenty. A rich, hydrating cream quickly plumps up fine, dry lines and reflects light, giving the appearance of a complexion that looks healthy – not pore parched!
- Invest in an illuminating lotion. It injects an immediate glow into the skin without looking obvious. Mix a pea-size amount of shimmer into a quarter-size amount of

your moisturiser and apply for a subtle sheen.

- Think flushed-up pink. A pretty pink blush instantly perks up your face and gives a fatigued-looking skin a run-in-the-park glow. Smile into the mirror (don't grimace) and gently pat and blend into the apples of your cheeks.
- Don't even think about using black eye liner. It will draw attention to puffiness and make eyes look piggy. A very light pencil in a neutral colour such as a very light blue run along close to the upper lash line is a clever way to counteract glassy, bloodshot eyes.
- Keep lips looking soft and natural with a slick of sheer gloss. Psychologically a bright pout can be too much to face and a shade that 'pops' will only highlight the sallowness of your skin.

CHAPTER 4

Canapés and desserts

We've worked out that your party can be as relaxed as you want it to be – if you want to spotlight your night in as a Takeaway Curry Night and stand back from the kitchen, for example, then go for it. But for those who want to complement their fancy drinks with fancy canapés, then this chapter is especially for you. The great thing is that you don't even have to be a brilliant cook (just a brilliant shopper) to pull off food that looks classy as well as, more importantly, edible. Canapés are also good fun to make, as the variations are limited only by your imagination.

Easy foodie short cuts

The art of throwing a night in so that you feel like a guest too, is wising up on the cheat tips. There are plenty of short cuts you can use so you're not stuck in a pinny all night. Here are just a few:

- Go for bite-sized nibbles. They look cute, they cut down on tableware (you only need napkins) and they're goof-proof to eat when you have a cocktail in your hand.
- Lay canapés out on a table on white or single-coloured plates. Patterns detract from the food's wow factor and can make nibbles look messy and off-putting.
- Make the majority of your canapés cold, as they can be prepared in advance and add up to fuss-free entertaining.
- For smart supermarket buys look to cold flans that you can cut up in advance into bite-size

pieces, and cocktail sausages served with a mustard dip on the side, as well as an assortment of cheeses, crackers, olives and nuts.

- Serve up platters of delicious hams and salamis. Buy the best quality meat you can and serve alongside fresh chunky bread.

- Fill salads bowls with fresh rocket, Parmesan shavings and cherry tomatoes drizzled with balsamic vinegar.

- If throwing your party during the winter, I think it's always nice to have a big saucepan of soup (buy freshly made) simmering on the stove. Serve in tea cups and save on the spoons.

- Make up a huge platter of sandwiches and transform them into fancy finger food by cutting off the crusts (who cares if your hair doesn't curl?) and arrange them artistically. Make them the afternoon of the party and cover well with clingfilm so that they don't dry out and harden at the edges.

Clueless about canapés?

For those of you who actively come out in hives when faced with cooking, rest assured that canapés are simply anything spread on a base. Canapés are usually made from small squares of bread or toast, but you can easily expand on this idea and use pitta bread or rye bread for a healthier base. Alternatively, why use bread at all? Strong baby salad leaves such as chicory, as well as tortilla chips and various robust vegetables all make for good bite-size savoury carriers. If you've got time you can always roast brightly coloured vegetables in the oven and drizzle olive oil over the top.

TOP TOPPINGS

For the canapé-challenged here are a few basics you can add to your shopping list and pop on top of your canapés:

anchovies	finely chopped nuts
bacon bits	olives
capers	pimientos
caviar	sliced radishes
cheese	shrimps
crab meat	cherry tomatoes

PARTY POOPER Serving canapés that are too big and fussy. Guests don't want to do battle with complicated food.

PARTY SOOTHER Serving nibbles that can be enjoyed in one, or at the most, two bites. Any more is a sit-down meal!

Life beyond cheese and pineapple sticks

You don't want your food looking like leftovers from a bad-taste wedding, so try to do something a little bit different so everyone will be delightfully surprised. It will make you feel good, too. Offering freshly prepared food instead of the usual tasteless nibbles that are available at a deep freeze near you makes for the Domestic Goddess factor. Here are some sassy and tasty little recipes you can whip up fast. Let's kick off with the hotties:

BRUSCHETTA
This is an Italian garlic toast and is a great alternative to garlic bread.

Serves 4
You will need
4 slices of bread
1 garlic clove
4 tablespoons olive oil
salt

Cook it up
1 *Toast the bread on both sides under until a grill until golden. Peel the garlic and cut in half. Rub the cut sides of the garlic over the toasted bread.*

2 *Drizzle the olive oil over the garlic toasts, season with salt and serve while warm.*

3 *To perk up your bruschettas you can also top up with ingredients such as mature brie with black olive tapenade, sun-blushed tomatoes and rocket or mozzarella with chopped cherry tomatoes and fresh basil.*

SCRUMMY SHREDDED BEEF TORTILLAS

Prepare the beef and pepper the day before to cut down your prep time. Adjust the recipe depending on how many people you have.

Serves 4

You will need
2 tortilla wraps
2 teaspoons sesame oil
1 small red or yellow pepper, deseeded and cut into strips
175 g/6 oz beef fillet sliced into long, thin strips
25 g/1 oz beansprouts
2 teaspoons sesame seeds
1 teaspoon cornflower
125 ml/4 fl oz/½ cup teriyaki marinade and sauce

Cook it up
1 *Preheat the oven to 110° C/225° F/Gas ¼. Sprinkle the tortillas with a little water and warm in the oven for a couple of minutes.*

2 *Heat the sesame oil in a large frying pan. When hot, add the pepper strips and stir-fry for 2 minutes. Add the beef and stir-fry for another minute.*

3 *Add the beansprouts and sesame seeds, and continue to stir-fry for another minute. Mix the cornflower with the teriyaki marinade, then pour this over the beef mixture. Allow to cook for another minute and then remove from the heat.*

4 *Divide the stir-fry between the tortillas, roll up and slice. Use the remaining sauce as a dip.*

LA LA LAND PIZZA
A pre-made bought base is essential for quickness. You can add whatever topping you like, but I quite like these California-style ingredients.

Serves 8 (bite-sized pieces)
You will need
1 pre-made pizza base lightly smeared with tomato sauce your choice of toppings. I suggest onions, garlic, pesto, goat's cheese, pine nuts, peppers, mozzarella, aubergine, anchovies, capers and black olives.

Cook it up
Preheat the oven to 220°C/425°F/Gas 7. On your base add sautéed sliced onions (you can fry them hours beforehand). Bake for 20 minutes. Cut into mini-sized pieces.

ULTRA-QUICK KEBABS

These take about 15 minutes to prepare and about 8 minutes to cook. Rope in a friend to help.

Serves 8

You will need

300 g/10½ oz minced lamb
1 medium egg, beaten
1 small onion, finely chopped
2 garlic cloves, crushed
1 red chilli, finely chopped
½ teaspoon ground cumin
2 tablespoons finely chopped fresh mint
2 tablespoons finely chopped fresh parsley
250 g/9 oz Greek yogurt
1 tablespoon ready-made mint sauce
1 teaspoon honey
salt and freshly ground black pepper
1 teaspoon lemon juice, to serve

Cook it up

1 Place the minced lamb in a bowl and add the egg, onion, garlic, chilli and cumin. Stir well until combined. Add the mint and parsley and season well.

2 Split the mixture into 15-18 balls and thread onto skewers (a maximum of three balls per skewer). Mix the yogurt with the mint sauce and honey. Place the kebabs under the grill and cook for about 8 minutes, or until the juices run clear. Served with minted yogurt and a squeeze of lemon.

CHILLI PRAWNS

Prawns take minutes to stir-fry and they can be served cold.

Cook it up

Stir-fry large-sized prawns in a wok with a little chilli powder until pink. Serve in a bowl with chilli sauce and cocktail sticks to hand. Prepare a generous amount of the prawns as they are very more-ish!

Feed them without cooking

If you're not keen on cooking, or it's too hot to sizzle in the kitchen, try at these tasty snacks.

SMOKED SALMON TORTILLA WHEELS

Easy, quirky and can be prepared in advance. Simply pop them into the fridge and take out minutes before serving.

Serves 12
You will need
2 large tortillas
200 g/7 oz cream cheese
leaves from a round lettuce
200 g/7 oz smoked salmon
squeeze of lemon juice
freshly ground black pepper

Cook it up

1 *Spread the tortillas evenly with the cream cheese. Lay the lettuce leaves in a single layer on top of the cheese and press lightly to flatten.*

2 *Lay the slices of smoked salmon on top of the lettuce in an even layer. Squeeze over a little lemon juice and season with black pepper.*

3 *Tuck an edge under and roll the pancake as tightly as you can. Wrap with clingfilm and place in the fridge to firm up. To serve, cut into 1 cm/½ in slices.*

CUTE CUCUMBER AND TUNA NIBBLES
These are hassle-free to prepare and look good on a plate.

Serves 12
You will need
200 g/7 oz canned tuna, drained and flaked
1-2 tablespoons olive oil
handful of fresh chopped parsley
squeeze of lemon juice
½ small red onion, finely chopped
2 tablespoons olives, finely chopped
1 tablespoon capers or 2 anchovies, finely chopped
1 cucumber
salt and freshly ground black pepper

Cook it up

1 *Mix the tuna with the olive oil, parsley, lemon juice and red onion. Season with salt and pepper.*

2 *Add the olives, capers or anchovies. Cut the cucumber into 1 cm/1/2 in thick slices and place small spoonfuls of the mixture on top of each one.*

PEACH, STILTON AND PARMA HAM WRAPS

You can make as many as you like of these. They always go down well and take seconds to make.

Serves 16

You will need
fresh or canned peaches (in natural juice)
stilton cheese (blue cheese)
8 slices Parma ham
olive oil, for drizzling
salt and freshly ground black pepper

Cook it up

1 *Cut the peaches into fairly thick wedges, then slice the Stilton to about the same size.*

2 *Place a peach wedge and piece of Stilton together and wrap in half a strip of Parma ham. Season and then drizzle over some olive oil.*

EGG 'N' OLIVE SPREAD

Traditional but tasty. Serve with your canapé base of choice.

Serves 12

You will need

6 hard-boiled eggs, finely chopped
2 tablespoons mayonnaise
75 g/2¾ oz finely chopped green olives
2 teaspoons prepared horseradish
bread, toast, pitta bread or rye bread squares
salt and freshly ground black pepper

Cook it up

Stir all the ingredients together until well mixed. Chill until ready to spread onto your chosen canapé base.

Dips that make you go mmm!

Bowls of dips always go down well. Crudités aka veggie dippers can be anything you like from thickly sliced fennel to cucumber, celery and peppers. Why not add whole radishes and scrubbed baby carrots, too?

EFFORTLESS HUMMUS

This is the quickest and tastiest hummus ever.
Serves 8

You will need
1 can of chickpeas, drained
2 tablespoons tahini
1 tablespoon lemon juice
½ clove garlic, crushed
2–3 tablespoons olive oil (to achieve smooth texture)
salt and pepper
pitta bread, to serve

Cook it up
1 Mash the chickpeas. Stir with the other ingredients until well mixed.

2 Chill until ready to serve with warm pitta bread.

CREAMY AVOCADO DIP
Don't mix up this avocado dip until almost ready to serve, as although it contains lemon juice it will still oxidise a little.

Serves 12
You will need
4 ripe avocados
6 tablespoons sour cream
2 garlic gloves, peeled
¼ sweet onion, chopped
2 teaspoons lemon juice
salt and cayenne pepper to taste

Cook it up

1 *Scoop out the avocado flesh and put it into a blender. Pulse to chop roughly and then add the cream, garlic, onion and salt.*

2 *Continue pulsing until the mixture is smooth and the texture like thick yogurt. Add the cayenne pepper and lemon juice to spice it up.*

TRADITIONAL SALSA
The Spanish word for 'sauce' this dip certainly gives extra zip to the humble corn chip.

Serves 8–10
You will need
4 medium tomatoes, peeled and roughly chopped
1 large onion, finely chopped
4 celery sticks, finely chopped
1 green pepper, finely chopped
90 ml/3 fl oz/6 tablespoons olive oil
2 tablespoons finely chopped green chillies (remove the seeds first if you don't want it too hot)
juice of 1 lemon
1 teaspoon mustard
1–2 tablespoons chopped fresh coriander
1 teaspoon salt

Cook it up
Combine all the ingredients and chill before serving.

For girlfriends who are (always) slimming

There are always girlfriends watching their weight so stop them banging on about their hips/waist/thighs by catering for them with nibbles that are not too calorie laden – just don't tell them how many calories there are in a cocktail!

QUAIL'S EGGS
Dinky, cute little eggs that have funky marbled shells. They are lovely when boiled and served with some sea salt and black pepper. Simply boil the eggs for 1 minute 45 seconds and plunge them into cold water before shelling.

CELERY STICKS
Mix some blue cheese with enough low-fat mayonnaise to achieve a thick, creamy consistency. Spread it on sticks of celery. Cut the celery into 2.5 cm/1 in long pieces and top off with a walnut half.

PARSNIP CRISPS
Preheat the oven to 140° C/275° F/Gas 1. Peel thin strips of parsnip with a vegetable peeler and place on a baking sheet. Season with sea salt and freshly ground black pepper. Bake them for 45 minutes, or until they are dry and crisp.

LOW-FAT TZATZIKI

Lovely and refreshing, and good for you too!

Serves 8
You will need
200 g/7oz low-fat Greek-style yogurt
2 tablespoons very finely chopped cucumber
2 garlic cloves, crushed
handful of chopped mint
crudités, to serve

Cook it up
1 *Mix the yogurt, cucumber and garlic together to make a paste-like dip.*

2 *Add mint to taste and serve in a dish in the middle of a plate of crunchy, delicious crudités sliced into 5 cm/2 in sticks.*

PARTY POOPER Not having enough food. Always be generous with your servings. No guest should go home via a fast-food joint with a rumbling stomach.

PARTY SOOTHER If you haven't got enough china, don't worry. Unlike plastic cups, paper plates don't take away from the taste of the food.

Delicious desserts

In this section I thought that all I would suggest would be copious amounts of ice cream. But upon further girlie investigation I've discovered that an UGNI wouldn't be complete without a few guilty pleasures – namely desserts that run into three-figure calorie numbers. Let's be brutally honest here, the one time you can really enjoy dessert is with your girlfriends. When out on a date you always wind up skipping the third course as playing footsie under the table usually signals for something more exciting than just staying for the cheesecake!

Just like canapés, desserts don't have to heat up the kitchen. Something creamy, juicy and totally sinful can be whipped up the night before your night in and served with a professional flourish and an indulgent smile straight from the fridge.

STRAWBERRY FOOL

Any fruit will do really, but strawberries always seem that bit more girlie. Keep some clean glasses back to spoon the fool into.

Serves 8
You will need
225 g/8 oz strawberries
225 g/8 oz fromage frais
115 g/4 oz crème fraîche (or for the naughty, think double cream)

Cook it up
1 *Crush the strawberries with a fork in a bowl.*

2 *Fold in the fromage frais and crème fraîche or cream slowly but thoroughly. Chill before serving.*

BOOZY VODKA JELLY

You can use any flavour of vodka for this jelly. The only thing you have to do here is boil the kettle and make it the night before.

Serves 6
You will need
10 leaves of gelatine
250 g/9 oz caster sugar
4 strips lemon or lime peel
450 ml/16 fl oz flavoured vodka

Cook it up

1 *Immerse the gelatine leaves in a bowl of water. Leave for 10 minutes until they are soft.*

2 *In the bowl put the sugar and the lemon or lime peel and pour over 350 ml/12 fl oz boiling water. Dissolve by stirring and leave for a few minutes. Take out the peel.*

3 *Squeeze out the gelatine leaves to remove any surplus water. Tip the water away. To the warm sugar mix, add the gelatine leaves and dissolve by stirring. Add the vodka. Into a 20 fl oz/I pint jelly mould pour your boozy mixture. Chill for 3 to 4 hours. Flip the jelly out of the mould and serve with cream or ice cream.*

SUPER SUMMER PUDDING
Delicious served with cream. But remember this isn't a pudding to be whipped up at the last minute; it needs to be made the night before.

Serves 8
You will need
8 slices of white bread with crusts removed
225 g/8 oz blackcurrants
280 g/10 oz redcurrants
350 g/12 oz raspberries
175 g/6 oz caster sugar

Cook it up

1 *Line a 1.7 litre/3 pint pudding basin with the bread, leaving some to cover the top of the fruit.*

2 *Remove the stalks from the fruit and place in a saucepan with 2 tablespoons water and the sugar. Cook gently until the juice becomes a rich purple-red, usually about 7 minutes.*

3 *While the fruit is still warm, spoon into the basin and cover with the remainder of the bread. Put a plate on top and press down with a heavy weight (such as scale weights or a can). Put the basin on a plate and leave overnight in the fridge. Turn the pudding out onto a plate before serving.*

TOO TASTY TIRAMISU

This is so much simpler to make than it sounds and looks. It really is very easy to rustle up and is bake free. (Don't serve it to your pregnant girlfriends though, as it contains alcohol and raw eggs.)

Serves 12

You will need
5 tablespoons instant coffee
250 g/9 oz savoiardi (Italian sponge finger biscuits)
2 eggs
500 g/1lb 2oz mascarpone
75 g/2 ¾oz icing sugar
25 g/1 oz cocoa powder

Cook it up

1 *Make the coffee with 225 ml/8 fl oz hot water. Lay the biscuits out on a tray and soak them in the coffee.*

2 *Separate the eggs and mix the yolks into the mascarpone with the icing sugar. Beat the egg whites until soft peaks form and fold into the mascarpone mixture.*

3 *Place a layer of moistened biscuits into a ceramic or glass dish and cover with a thick layer of mascarpone mixture. Shake over some cocoa powder, then repeat with a further layer of biscuits and mascarpone mixture. Finish off with a dusting of cocoa powder and chill.*

DRAMA QUEEN PAVLOVA

My personal favourite and perfect for the Hen Night, as it looks just like a wedding cake!

Serves 6

You will need

selection of mixed fruits, such as kiwis, strawberries, peaches and blueberries
large amounts of whipping cream
2 large, ready-made meringue bases

Cook it up

1 *Peel, de-stalk and generally prepare the fruit. Whip up the cream.*

2 *Fold the fruit into the cream and spoon half of it into a*

83

meringue case. Place the second meringue case on top and spoon in the remaining cream and fruit.

CHOCOLATE STRAWBERRIES
Buy plenty of fresh strawberries and dip them into melting chocolate. Allow to cool and place on a dish. Delicious!

SIMPLE EXOTIC FRUITS
Marinate pieces of tropical fruits such as mango, pineapple and melon in Grand Marnier and stab on a skewer.

FUNKY FRUIT SALAD
Make as big or as small as you like.

Serves 6–8
You will need
apples, cored and sliced
mandarins or satsumas, peeled and segmented
fresh peaches, stoned and sliced
fresh pineapple rings cut into chunks
grapes
strawberries, hulled
200 ml/7 fl oz apple juice
200 ml/7 fl oz orange juice

Cook it up

1 *Core and slice the apples into small pieces and put into a bowl. Add the mandarins or satsumas, the peaches, pineapple, grapes and strawberries.*

2 *You can add any other fruity favourites at this point, such as banana, kiwi or melon. Mix the apple and orange juices together and add to the salad. Chill and serve dribbled with cream.*

On your dessert list

- Buy fun-sized bars of chocolate or tubes of Smarties and pour into a big bowl. Leave on the table so guests can unwrap at their leisure.
- Buy mini tubs of ice cream in various delicious and exotic flavours.
- Buy nice biscuits/Turkish delight/posh chocolates to serve with coffee. It makes the sobering-up experience far more tasteful.
- Colourful cup cakes like fondant fancies always look good. Borrow a cake stand from gran and serve in old-fashioned hotel style. A selection of teas will go down well at The Baby Shower.

The best baked cakes

You can't beat a home-made cake so how about baking a batch for your friends?

FAIRY CAKES

There's something magical about fairy cakes. They always get an excited aah! And they look pretty, too.

Makes 24 mini cakes
You will need
125 g/4¹/₂ oz softened butter
125 g/4¹/₂ oz caster sugar
2 eggs, lightly beaten
1 teaspoon vanilla extract
125 g/4¹/₂ oz self-raising flour
2 tablespoons milk
175 g/6 oz icing sugar
sugar decorations
bun tin and mini paper cases

Cook it up
1 *Preheat the oven to 190° C/375° F/Gas 5. Put 24 baking cases into a bun tin.*

2 *In a mixing bowl beat the butter and sugar until pale and fluffy (you can use an electric whisk to save your arm). Add the beaten eggs a little at a time, whisking as you go. Add the vanilla extract.*

3 *Sift in half the flour and fold into the mixture with a spoon. Add the milk a little at a time, folding in as you go along with the rest of the flour until well mixed.*

4 *Spoon the mixture into the mini paper cases and bake for about 10 minutes, or until risen and golden in colour. Leave to cool. To make the icing add a little water to the icing sugar and stir until thick and smooth but of a pourable consistency. Drizzle over the cakes. Decorate as you please.*

MINI CHOCOLATE CAKES
Totally adorable and truly scrumptious. Leave yourself half an hour to prepare them.

Makes about 30 cakes
You will need
450 g/1 lb chopped dark chocolate
450 g/1 lb unsalted butter
5 medium eggs
5 egg yolks
225 g/8 oz caster sugar
25 g/1 oz plain flour
1/2 teaspoon baking powder
flaked chocolate or cocoa, to dust

Cook it up
1 *Preheat the oven to 180° C/350° F/Gas 4. Put the chocolate and butter in a medium bowl and place over a pan of simmering water. Leave to melt for 20 minutes.*

2 *In another bowl, whisk the eggs, egg yolks and sugar until pale. Stir the melted chocolate and butter until smooth, then fold into the whisked eggs. Fold in the flour until completely mixed. Spoon the chocolate mixture into non-stick mini muffin tins and bake for 10 minutes, or until the cakes have risen and set. Leave to cool and then dust with chocolate flakes or cocoa.*

PARTY POOPER Boring everyone by saying 'do you know how many calories is in that?'

PARTY SOOTHER Hiring a chocolate fountain so guests can dip marshmallows whenever they feel like it through the evening.

CHAPTER 5

Party games

Remember the games you used to play at parties when you were a kid? Musical chairs, pass the parcel and blind man's bluff? Isn't it telling that you remember these games along with the fun/tears/tantrums more than the birthday cake or the presents themselves? It's a shame that a bunch of five-year-olds can experience more pant-wetting laughs at a single birthday party than many adults do all year. So why let the fun stop because you should be old enough to know better? Party games are tons of fun and can really make your night in come alive – they're also a great ice-breaker if you're inviting a gaggle of girls who aren't too familiar with each other. To make your night in rock put on your Game Girl hat and organise games that will make everybody look as silly as each other. You may want to take a group oath that no secrets or embarrassing stories be uttered beyond your four walls!

Frolics for everyone

These games will be suitable for any giggly occasion.

FAME GAME

This is a nice gentle one to get started with and a blast to play. The day before the party flick through a stack of magazines and cut out celebrities – they can be sports stars, film stars, singers, reality stars and C-list celebrities! Then fold the pictures up and put them into a bowl. Each round is limited to just half a minute, so have a watch with a second hand ready. The first girl to pull a picture out of the bowl tries to get the girl on her left to guess the celebrity. After the famous name is guessed, the clue giver can continue pulling pictures out of the bowl for another 30 seconds. Here are the rules:

- The clue giver can talk, but no pointing.
- She can't spell out the person's name. But she can give the initials of their names.
- She can give clues around the person's name. For instance, if the name is Madonna, she can say 'it's a religious icon.'
- The clue guesser notches up a point for each of the names that she guesses correctly in the time.
- The turn then passes to the guesser who now becomes the clue giver, and her neighbour becomes the new celebrity detective.

TRUTH OR DARE

Now, I've mentioned Truth or Dare earlier on in the cocktail section, where I said the truth part of this game can usually be a bit lame, and so I suggested Drink or Dare as an alternative. But what I didn't mention is that after a few strong cocktails while playing Drink or Dare the truth will start to out itself. This is where the game starts to get very, very interesting! So, gather your girlie guests into a group and fire the questions.

Ten taster questions for truth

1. If you could date any of your girlfriends' boyfriends, who would it be and why?
2. Which relationship appeals to you more: a wild passionate one or a quiet and calm one? Which one are you in?
3. How many times have you fallen for ex-sex (that's sleeping with your boyfriend after you've split up)?
4. If you could be a fly on a bedroom wall, which famous couple would you choose?
5. Would you sleep with your boss to get the job you want?
6. What's the biggest lie you've ever told? And to whom?
7. What is the most annoying and embarrassing habit a partner of yours has ever had?
8. If you knew the end of the world was in an hour, what would be the last thing that you would do?
9. Love or lust? What's most important to you?
10. How far would you go to earn a million?

Ten to-die-for dares

1. Fake a convincing orgasm à la *When Harry Met Sally*.
2. Eat something from the rubbish bin.
3. Serenade someone in the group – passionately.
4. Attempt to stand on your head.
5. Wear one of the group's knickers on your head.

6. Sing a song with a mouthful of cake.
7. Floss your teeth in front of everyone.
8. Do the cancan.
9. Stick your head out of the living room window and shout as loud as you can into the street 'I am cupid, I will find you love!'.
10. Run down the street wearing just your underwear.

PARTY POOPER Not joining in.

PARTY SOOTHER Have a Polaroid camera ready with plenty of film to snap disgusted/surprised/drunk faces.

NAME THAT TUNE

A much tamer game, but still fun. You will need a CD player and some compact discs with compilations of songs – they can even be related to your theme night. Play the first few bars and see which guest can name that tune the fastest. Keep track of the points; you could even present the winner with the CD.

MAKE THEM LAUGH

As a fan of comedy clubs I think there's no better way to spend an evening than laughing until your sides are splitting. Why not brief everybody on your invite to get together a five-minute stand-up comedy routine? It can either be something they've totally made up themselves or a monologue that they've memorised from a comedienne such as Victoria Wood. Make it professional by clearing a little stage area, getting a mike and plugging it into your amplifier, and acting as compère by introducing them.

Hula Hoop

This isn't just for kids. After a few drinks it's hilarious. Hula hoops are really cheap to buy – so why not get a few and hold a 'hula' contest? It's the best waist-shaper exercise about, too.

TWO TRUTHS V ONE LIE

Everyone sits in a circle and takes turns telling three things about themselves and their lifestyle. One of them is a whopping, great lie. For example:

1. I once went out with my ex-boyfriend's brother.
2. I never wear white knickers.
3. I once had a cat that ate my goldfish and was then killed by my dog

Everyone then has to guess and vote on which is the lie. It's really funny to see what people come up with for their lie, plus you learn a lot of funny truths – even from your oldest friends.

'CAN YOU IMAGINE' GAME

Again, everyone sits in a circle where each girl has a piece of paper and a pen. Each girl then thinks of a silly sentence to write on the paper. Your sentence should start with the words: 'Can you imagine…' Try to be as creative/ridiculous/funny as you can. For example a good one is, 'Can you imagine if my boyfriend wore false teeth? Or 'Can you imagine if the letter S didn't exist in the alphabet?' Then each person passes their paper to the right and answers the question they were handed. The answers could be something like: 'I'd use them as a pair of castanets and dance around the room', or 'I would never be able to ask for sex again.' Once everyone has finished answering their question, start with one girl in your circle and go to the right. The first person reads the 'Can You Imagine' question and the person to their right reads the answer they wrote for the question handed to them. So it would be: Can you imagine if my boyfriend had false teeth? I would never be able to ask for sex again.' Then the person who just read their answer now reads her question and the person on her right reads their answer until you finish the circle.

Oh mummy! Games for the Baby Shower

Baby showers can be looked upon as boring – after all the mum-to-be can't drink. But throw in a few games and things begin to liven up. These games are guaranteed to get everybody giggling.

KEEPING MUM

Each girl receives a dummy when she arrives. Explain to the girls' only once: if you catch someone saying the word 'baby' you get to take her dummy. The one with the most dummies at the end of the shower has kept mum and wins a gift.

WHO'S THAT GIRL?

Tell each guest to bring a photo of herself when she was a baby. Pin them up and have the guests try to pick who's who.

WHAT'S IN THE BAG?

Put lots of things that relate to pregnancy and babies into a bag. They can be things like a dummy, breast pads, breast pump, large knickers, a nursing bra, and so on. Then, in turn, get each person to put her hand into the bag without looking (blindfold her) and feel an item. She then has to try to guess what it is.

GUESS THE GOO!

Buy six jars of different types of baby foods and empty into separate bowls so that nobody knows which is which – except you. Write the flavour onto a sticker at the bottom of the bowl. Everyone present has to taste the food in each bowl and write down what she thinks it is.

FEED THE (BIG) BABY

Have girls partner up. Put a bib on one person in each team. Have the other person get behind her to be her 'arms'. The person behind feeds the person with the bib from a jar of baby food. The first pair to finish their food wins. This can get messy and funny, so have the camera ready.

Games for a hilarious hen night

If you're holding a hen night in then it needs to be just as much fun as if you were holding it in a bar. So drink should be free-flowing and games daft but fun.

THE WEDDING DRESS GAME

The guests are divided up into several groups and given a roll of toilet paper. The teams are told they must create a wedding dress using only the one roll of toilet paper. One member of the team becomes the bride-to-be and the rest decorate. The real bride-to-be will judge the results.

WHO KNOWS THE SECRETS OF THE BRIDE?

As the hostess you need to be in cahoots with the bride before the party. Come up with 15 questions together about the bride and her groom that will lead to stories about the nearly wedded happy couple. For each question have the correct answer along with three incorrect answers. Before you play, organise the questions from easy to difficult, and then give each guest a pen and paper. The first question is read out by you, with the four possible answers. Each guest writes down what she believes is the correct answer. Now everyone shows the answer they have selected. The bride reveals the correct one and those who answer correctly continue to play. To make the game more personal, the bride can expand on the question – how they first met, for example, and what they thought of each other – before continuing with the next question. The winner wins a mystery gift in a nicely wrapped box.

HE SAID, SHE SAID

This time the hostess needs to be in cahoots with the groom. Call him before the party and ask him about ten questions, such as: '[Insert your own bride-to-be's name] fancies giving you a sexy night in. She raids the cupboard for chocolate spread, but has run out. What does she choose instead?' The groom has to answer the question with his bride-to-be in mind. At the party you then ask the bride the same questions and see if her answers match her groom's. Will they be a perfect match?

TELL ME A STORY

Make a list of everything the bride-to-be might say while opening her wedding gifts. For example: 'Ooh, aah, that's a big one, I've never seen one like that before, I've got two of those, that's a dinky size ...' you get the picture? Next, each person has to make up a quick story about the bride's wedding night based on these comments. It can be absolutely side splitting.

THE SILLY SOCK GAME

Blindfold the player and hand her a pillow case filled with old (clean) socks. The aim of the game is put as many pairs of socks on your hands as you can in just one minute. The person who manages to get the most pairs on wins. The giggle factor of this game is that after managing to put on the first pair you have lost the use of your fingers and can't feel what you're doing.

KEEP YOUR KNICKERS ON!

Everybody has to buy a pair of pants and wrap them up. Each guest then chooses a pant parcel and then takes off her own knickers and wear the ones she has chosen. The fun in this is not wearing run-of-the-mill pants but outrageous ones. So buy old granny pants, Bridget Jones tummy-tightening pants, sexy pants from Agent Provocateur, and so on.

THE CATWALK CAPER

This is perfect for fashionistas for the Heels and High Jinks night in. It's a lot like dressing up – but in a grown up kind of way, naturally! Have your girls bring round their sexiest/slinkiest dresses along with a heap of accessories: high shoes, hats, feather boas, sunglasses, wigs, and so on, and put on a catwalk show. Get each girl to dress up to the nines. For the soundtrack include Duran Duran's 'Girls On Film' and 'The Model' by Kraftwerk, and get catwalking. Once swaggering down the runway (the middle of your room) your model will be greeted by cheers, claps and whoops from fellow girlfriends. To help with your steps take note that the word 'catwalk' is actually jazz terminology meaning you walk like a cat, in other words slinky. To achieve this cross one leg in front of the other. No walking like a policewoman!

How to strut like a model

1. Lengthen your spine and lift your chin.
2. Place your hands low on your hips.
3. Walk like a peacock and stick your chest out.
4. Overlap your feet as you walk to give your hips a sway
5. Imagine there's a hand pushing you in the small of your back. This will tilt your shoulders back.
6. Do not smile. Catwalk models never smile.

The hot-card shuffle poker night

··

The girls' biggest deal! There's little doubt that poker has become sexy. It's now been outed as the card game to be seen playing. And let's just say it sorts the women out from the girls! It's a game of skill, memory and strategy, which can be exhilarating, punishing and even humiliating. To hold your own poker night, it's best to invite girls who know or are willing to read up on the rules before they come – to outline them here would demand a book in itself. But poker, at its very essence, is a simple game. Its countless versions can be quite complex, but a popular one (in cowboy films anyway) is five-card stud. For more suggestions go to www.pokernews.com.

UNDERSTANDING THE CARDS

Poker is played with a standard deck of 52 cards. The cards are ranked from high to low in the following order: ace, king, queen, jack, 10, 9, 8, 7, 6, 5, 4, 3, 2. Aces are always high. Aces are worth more than kings, which are worth more than queens, which are worth more than jacks, and so on. The cards are also separated into four suits. They are: clubs, spades, hearts and diamonds. (see page 13 for the various hands.)

A POKER VIRGIN'S GUIDE TO PLAYING TEXAS HOLD 'EM

If you're a newcomer to poker then Texas Hold 'Em is for you. It's the most commonly played poker game and easy to pick up. Hold 'Em is perfect for a small girlie gathering too, as it can be played with as few as two players. The Poker Cheat Sheet on page 13 contains a list of hands so that you will know which hand is strongest. And don't forget, Aces are high. The aim of the game is to make the best five card hand using a combination of one or both of the cards in your hand and the community cards on the table. You can bet because you think you have the strongest hand, or you may want to bluff and pretend you have the strongest hand.

THE 12 STEP (SIMPLE) RULES
1. One girl is initially chosen as the dealer although she will also be playing the game (in the next round the dealer will be the person to the current dealer's left and so on). She shuffles up a complete pack of playing cards.
2. Antes are usually used in Hold 'Em in which the two players to the left of the dealer place out a previously agreed amount of money (or choco-lates/beads/matchsticks) into the pot. The 'small

blind' (to the left of the dealer) puts down half the amount of the 'big blind' (second the left of the dealer). This is called 'posting the blinds'.

3. Okay, it's now time for the dealer to deal each player two cards facing them downwards. These are known as your 'hole' cards.

4. Now's the time for a round of betting beginning with the girl to the left of the two players who posted the blinds.

5. Players can then decide whether to check, raise or fold. Check this essential poker terminology in the box!

6. Betting continues (including the dealer) until everyone has called and each player has same amount of money in the pot, or has folded.

7. The dealer then turns over three cards onto the table. This is known as the 'flop'. These are the community cards which you will use to conjure up your best hand along with your two hole cards. Time to bet once more starting with the player to the left of the dealer.

8. After all betting is completed, the dealer turns over another card onto the table. This fourth card is known as the 'turn' card. A betting round follows.

9. The dealer then places a final community card up on the table. This fifth card is known as the 'river'.

YOUR AT-A-GLANCE GUIDE TO POKER TERMS

Ante A compulsory stake before the deal

Blind The compulsory bet or bets to the dealer's left

Burns To discard the top card

Call To match a bet

Check Choosing not to bet (this can only be done if all players have the same amount in the pot excluding those who have folded)

Community Cards Cards on the table that can make up everyone's hands

Flop The first three community cards to be dealt face up onto the centre of the table

Fold To withdraw from the game or give up the hand

Hole Cards Cards dealt facedown which only the player given them can see

Pot The pile of money on the table combining the ante and the bets

Raise To call and increase the previous bet

River The fifth and final community card

Showdown The final revealing of the hole cards

Turn The fourth community card to be dealt. Also known as Fourth Street

105

You now have the opportunity to use any combination of the five cards on the table and your two hole cards to create your best five card poker hand.

10. Place your bets for the final time. Remember, betting is started with the player to the left of the dealer.

11. If a player raises the bet and the other players call or 'see' their hand then the person who raised the bet reveals their hand first.

12. Don't forget that there is no need to show your hand unless your hand beats the revealed cards.

PARTY POOPER Losing your car/house/man.

PARTY SOOTHER Walking away with the winnings.

The DVD (I'm-in-the-mood-for-a-movie) Night

As well as stacking up on the DVDs and the popcorn, why not organise a quiz for your movie buff girl-friends? As the movie hostess, think of about 50 movie trivia questions, hand out pen and paper and ask your girlfriends to write down the answers. The winner wins a DVD of her choice (each loser puts in a few pounds). Here are a few to get you started:

1. Who said 'I have a head for business and a body for sin. Is there anything wrong with that?'
2. What was the A-list girl clique in *Mean Girls* called?
3. What was Reese Witherspoon's very blonde character called in *Legally Blonde*?
4. What were the surnames of Harry and Sally in *When Harry Met Sally*?
5. Which movie is this immortal line from: 'Kiss me. Kiss me as if it were the last time'?
6. Who said this line and in what film: 'That's more than a dress. That's an Audrey Hepburn movie.'?

Sshh! Answers are: Melanie Griffith in *Working Girl*; The Plastics; Elle Woods; Harry Burns and Sally Albright; *Casablanca*; Tom Cruise to Renée Zellweger in *Jerry Maguire*.

CHAPTER 6

Chill out and relax

Not every UGNI has to be riotous, bawdy and full on. Sometimes when everyday stress gets too much for a girl to bear it's nice to gather an intimate group of girl-friends and just chill out – the emphasis being on winding down. An evening spent getting rid of the trappings and tensions of civilisation – yes, and that does include annoying boyfriends – can be priceless. Think of this girls' night in as the antidote to the Hen

Night where holistic treatments trade for drinking games, and positive relaxation takes over. Rest assured that this evening is all about self-indulgence where you let go of physical tension and calm right down. Fatigue won't floor you once you're armed with this chapter's instant rechargers.

Discover your dosha (my what?)

This is a really fun self-assessment test you can do at the beginning of your Chill Out and Relax evening and can put you and your girl gang onto the road to enlightenment. The revealed feelgood factor is also a good clue as to what treatment you can offer your girl-friends. Doshas are three distinct types of people that were identified by the Indians thousands of years ago and are the backbone of Ayurvedic medicine. Each dosha has positive and negative traits, and benefits from different treatments and diet. Find out which ones you and your girlfriends fall into.

WHAT'S YOUR DOSHA?

Write down your scores for the attributes below, then find out your dosha at the end of the list.

1 **How would you describe your physique?**

a. Tall or very short. Thin and bony. You find it hard to put on weight.

b. Of moderate height with good muscles.

c. Large and well developed. You find losing weight a problem.

2 **Your skin is:**

a. Dry, rough or thin.

b. Normal to sensitive.

c. Thick, oily and pale.

3 **If you skin is playing up, which are you most likely to suffer from?**

a. Flaking or tightness.

b. Spots.

c. Blackheads and open pores.

4 **How are your energy levels?**

a. Quick bursts of energy that burn and then flicker out.

b. Moderate to good energy bursts.

c. Lots of stamina and high levels of energy.

5 **Which of the following describes your nails?**

a. Brittle.

b. Strong and flexible.

c. Strong and inflexible.

6 How would you describe your temperament?

a. Nervous and sometimes oversensitive.

b. Highly motivated and passionate.

c. Loyal and calm in a crisis.

7 What type of weather don't you like?

a. The wind, and always feeling cold.

b. Blistering hot summer days.

c. Cold damp days.

8 How would you describe your appetite?

a. Variable, you can eat day or night.

b. You need good regular meals to stave off hunger.

c. You rarely feel hungry.

9 When stressed, you:

a. Get anxious, worried and can't sleep.

b. Get frustrated and lose your temper.

c. Feel calm but depressed.

10 Your speech is:

a. Fast and frequent.

b. Sharp and cutting.

c. Slow and melodious.

If you scored mostly A's you are **Vata**
If you scored mostly B's you are **Pitta**
If you scored mostly C's you are **Kapha**

YOUR DOMINANT DOSHA LOWDOWN

Now its time to discover what your dosha means for you:

Vata
You are imaginative, quick witted and like to get things done quickly without fuss. You worry excessively and tend to take on too much, which leads to stress and exhaustion.

You need to Slow down and learn to say no. Take time out for yourself to help you relax. Try meditation, t'ai chi or some other form of relaxation.

Best foods As you are affected by the cold, eat plenty of warm foods such as soups, stews and cooked vegetables.

Your feelgood factor A body massage to release all that tight tension.

Pitta
You are dynamic and passionate. You are the life and soul of the party and are a good planner. Therefore this is the perfect book for a hostess in the making!

However, you don't cope well under stress and can have a hot and explosive temper.

You need to Control your temper and learn to be more tolerant of other people's weaknesses and imperfections. Kick-boxing is an ideal sport for you to expel aggression.

Best foods You need foods that help balance moods. Eat plenty of fresh fruits, yogurts and green leafy vegetables. Avoid too many treats with a high sugar content, which can send your moods on a rollercoaster of highs and lows.

Your feelgood factor Lie down with an eye mask straight out of the fridge, slow down your breathing and teach yourself to tune out.

Kapha

You are solid and dependable, a steady worker and a good team player. By nature you are compassionate and caring. You are also laid back and don't get too stressed.

You need to Become more motivated. Laid back is good, but sluggish in mind and body, bad! On occasion you can fall into a rut, so you need to concentrate on boosting your energy levels.

Best foods Ensure that most of your calories come from carbohydrates and proteins rather than dairy and fatty foods. These can slow down the metabolism as well as your energy levels. Fresh fruits, pulses and vegetables are ideal.

Your feelgood factor Good, long stretches to energise and empower your mind.

Drinks that calm

This evening is all about calming down and rebalancing mind and body. So although cocktails aren't off the menu if you don't want them to be, a detoxifying or replenishing tonic could be just the thing your body needs – and it comes in the shape of a juicer along with a visit to the greengrocers. If you haven't got a juicer or a blender, ask a friend to bring hers along. For the best effect from the juices, prepare them just before you are ready to drink them as they will oxidise quite quickly. Prepare as much as possible beforehand – but don't core apples or peel bananas until the last minute.

CRANBERRY CLEANSER

A refreshing and flushing juice teeming with vitamins A and C, and potassium. The pectin in the pear will help remove toxins while cranberries are known for killing bacteria in the kidneys, bladder and urinary tract. Great if you suffer from cystitis.

You will need
1 pear
125 ml/4 fl oz/½ cup cranberry juice

Blend it up

Juice the pear and add to the cranberry juice. Serve in a tall glass over ice.

A KIWI KICK

Kiwi fruits are a nutritional powerhouse as they're loaded with vitamin C (more than oranges). By combining the two fruits you are giving yourself a double vitamin whammy.

The Power Juices

A glass of fresh juice is the ultimate nutrient-packed power drink, so blend up some of the suggestions below or make a signature concoction of your own. Here's the nutrient lowdown on the best juices.

- **Apple** Cleansing
- **Carrot** Revitalising
- **Beetroot** Blood purifier
- **Pineapple/papaya** Digestive tonic
- **Spinach** Eliminator (use young spinach only)
- **Lemon** Antibacterial
- **Celery** Nerve tonic
- **Watercress** Intestinal cleanser
- **Cabbage** Constipation cure
- **Grapes** Metabolism booster

Because vitamin C is a water-soluble vitamin, it's quickly lost from the body and needs replenishing daily.

You will need
2 large oranges, peeled
2 kiwi fruits, peeled

Blend it up
Peel the oranges. Juice with the kiwi fruits. Serve over ice.

GET HIGH ON WHEATGRASS!
Whizz up a wheatgrass health drink that's high in chlorophyll (the pigment in plants that converts sunlight into energy). Devotees say it does wonders for humans. You can buy the juice at health stores or, if you're dedicated then make it yourself. Buy the seeds and dutifully sow and water them. Once the grass has shooted simply cut a handful of wheatgrass close to the roots and process in a juicer. Be warned, it's an acquired taste, but you can add it to other fruit juices for a more palatable drink.

Health to a Tea

Go into any health spa and they will always offer you a tea. But not any old tea. Oh no, it's herbal tea. Why? Because herbal teas taste delicious, are calorie-free and contain no nasty stimulants such as caffeine or tannin.

(Tannin prevents the body from absorbing vital minerals from food.) Herbal teas are 100 per cent goodness and there is no limit to how many you can drink. Prepare to play mum, rinse out the teapot and pour one of the following:

Camomile Known as a 'ladies' herb, it relaxes the nervous system and is great to sip for period pains as it gently soothes and eases internal muscles.

Dandelion An excellent diuretic and a great brew for fluid retention. It can be drunk to kick-start sluggish kidneys and is also good for helping to clear up spots and blemishes by speeding up the removal of toxins.

Fennel A sweet and refreshing tea to help the overindulged. Clues are indigestion and flatulence!

Lemon Balm Primarily a relaxant and helps alleviate nervous tension, stress and insomnia.

Nettle Rich in vitamins and minerals, especially iron. Helps mineralise the body, stimulates blood circulation and improves kidney function.

Peppermint Wonderful for the digestion – hence the popularity of After Eights post meal! Clears the head and freshens the breath.

Rosehip A stimulating tea, which is rich in vitamin C. It's also great for warding off the sniffles.

Rosemary Said to lift spirits, quicken your memory and stimulate the senses. Great to drink if you're feeling 'heady'.

PARTY POOPER Serving herbal tea in a builder's mug. It spoils the delicate taste of the herbs!

PARTY SOOTHER Serving herbal teas in a cup and saucer or a tall glass.

The treatment menu

One of the pleasures of hosting a Chill Out and Relax evening is that it really throws everyone together in a most personal way! There's nothing nicer than sharing touch or even the same breath, such as when meditating with a group of girls you really care about – in fact the whole evening can have the effect of bringing you closer together. First up, your girlfriends and you should decide what treatments you fancy – you could even then draw up a rough rota of who's going to give what to whom. For example, a girlfriend who's had a tension headache all week would benefit from someone giving her an Indian head massage, or someone who's been pounding a computer keyboard for days would fall over with gratitude at being offered a hand massage, I'm sure.

To make the menu easy to get to grips with I've

grouped similar treatments together. You can dip in and out of and play around with them as much as you like. Firstly, there's the let's-do-it-altogether-girlie-bonding suggestions of meditation and yoga – simply move your furniture to one side to turn your room into a DIY chill-out studio. Alternatively, keep the furniture where it is and do facial yoga – it sure beats Botox! Then it's onto the massage section where neck, face, shoulders, hands and arms are each addressed. Once you've mastered the moves, you can then improvise as much as you like and even turn your attentions to the back, stomach and legs. Just like the massage movements, go with the flow of what your girlfriends' relaxation needs are. And to round off the chapter, you can dip into alternative therapies such as Indian head massage, reflexology and mystic hand signals.

Chill-out therapies

Look to the East for some traditional ways to find peace of mind along with a flexible body.

MEDITATION MADE EASY

Once upon a kooky time, meditation was seen just for the weird sandal brigade, but today the thinking is that a strong mind equals a strong body. Just ask Madonna who demands a special 'peace room' when she's on tour so that she can meditate before going on stage. The truth is, the modern meditator is more than likely to be a stressed out trying-to-juggle-it-all kind of girl than a Woodstock dropout – rather like Mrs Ritchie! Taking a more spiritual approach to life's dilemmas and making time for meditation goes towards healing and strengthening the immune system. You don't even have to adopt the lotus position to benefit. And what's more, meditation is said to help not only stress but also high blood pressure, anxiety and headaches, too.

Here's how to lose the tension

It's hard to go straight into Zen mode when you want to shout 'Aargh!' instead of chanting 'om'. Ease yourself into relaxation by first letting go of initial physical tension. I think it's a nice idea for the hostess to really take control here, so it's a thoughtful touch to record these instructions on a tape in a calming voice and play them back during the session.

1. Lie down, close your eyes and let your feet naturally flop outwards and your arms fall away from your body with palms facing upwards. Breathe gently but deeply.
2. Screw up your facial muscles and then let them

relax as if you skin is slipping to the floor.

3. Lift up your head and let it fall gently back. Relax your jaw and neck and feel your throat opening up.

4. Press your shoulders against the floor and then relax them. Fully stretch out your arms and fingers, holding them stiff for a few seconds before letting them go limp.

5. Lift your bottom off the floor and then let it fall, feeling your spine first stretch and then relax as you do so. Keeping your heels together, stretch your legs and wriggle your toes out, then relax them completely.

6. Stay relaxed for a few minutes and rise slowly. Your muscles should feel as floppy as a rag doll.

You need a Chill Out and Relax night in if:

- Lately you've been feeling on the verge of tears.
- You want to throw a vase, complete with water and flowers, at your boyfriend's head.
- Your concentration drifts off regularly.
- You're tired all the time (TATT).
- You worry about the next day, and the one after that.

How to have a meditation moment

Although it's often easier to get started with the help of an experienced teacher, there's nothing to stop you from learning a spot of DIY calm with friends in your own home. All it takes is a quiet room, 15 minutes and a touch of self-discipline – so that means no sniggering or giggling at the back of the room! Again, you as the hostess can record and play back the following during the session.

- Sit cross-legged (most people find it comfortable) with your head, neck and back straight, but not stiff (it's more comfortable with a cushion tucked just under your bottom near to the back, as this keeps your back straight, or you can sit with your back against a wall). Try to push away all thoughts of the past and future and just concentrate on the here and now.
- Become aware of your breathing, focusing on the sensation of air moving in and out of your body as you breathe. Feel your belly rise and fall as the air enters your nostrils and leaves your mouth. Pay attention to the way each breath changes and differs. As you become more relaxed it should slow down and become deeper.
- Once your breathing and therefore your body have fallen into a sedative state you are now ready

to 'read' your thoughts. When thoughts pop into your mind don't ignore or suppress them, simply note them, remain calm and use your breathing as an anchor. What you don't want to do is to be constantly thinking about all your annoying must-do chores, so let the thoughts drift in and then drift out again. Replace them with something calming – such as visualising a tropical beach scene. This will focus the mind away from everyday 'clutter'.

- Bring yourself slowly back to normal consciousness, sit for a minute or two and rise gradually.

Creating your place of calm

- Play Zero Seven or any chill-out compilation.
- Burn aromatherapy oils.
- Dim the lights or burn candles.
- Kick off shoes.
- Wear comfortable and loose clothing.
- Take the phone off the hook and switch off mobile phones.

At-home yoga

It's official, yoga makes you happier, calmer and yes, hotter! Just ask the slew of A-listers who make it part of their daily workouts: Madonna, Gwyneth, Jennifer Aniston et al. Yoga is the ultimate mind and body workout – think of it as a cross between a therapy session and a massage. The word yoga is also a Sanskrit word meaning 'union' which is kind of cool as you've got your girlfriends round. You can even record moves onto a tape and play them back to your girlfriends as you did with the meditation idea. So, take a deep breath, say 'om' and slip your body into of these three basic *asanas* (exercises in yoga speak). Keep up sweeties!

Cat stretch
Why do it? Purrfect for ridding the spine of tension.
1. Kneel on all fours with your hands on the floor in front of you. Place your knees directly under your hips and hands directly under your shoulders. Exhale and slowly arch your back into a hump, with your head dropped down and your tummy held in. Inhaling, slowly lift your head and at the same time gently drop your lower back and stick your bottom out. Repeat three times.
2. Gently bend your elbows and place your chin on the floor between your hands.

3. Slowly straighten your arms, lifting your head, and then take your left knee forward towards your forehead.

4. Lift your head, look up at the ceiling and, at the same time, move your left leg back and point your toe to the ceiling behind you. Repeat this movement three times and then switch over to the right leg.

The triangle

Why do it? Great for relieving stiffness in the lower back and for proper functioning of the digestive system.

1. Stand with feet shoulder width apart. Point your left foot to the left and your right foot also slightly to the left. Stretch your left arm out at shoulder level and bring the right arm straight up against your right ear. Inhale.

2. As you exhale, bend to the left and slightly forward to bypass your ribs. Slide your left hand down your left leg and hold onto the lowest part you can comfortably reach. Look up at your right hand. Take several deep breaths before releasing the postion. Repeat bending to the right.

Standing chest expansion

Why do it? This will relax the muscle at the back of the shoulders as well as firming your bust.

1. Stand and interlock your hands behind your back, keeping your elbows straight. Inhale and raise your arms as high as possible, holding for a count of five.

2. Exhale and gently fold into a forward bend, keeping knees slightly bent and dropping your head, neck and chest towards the floor, continuing to lift your arms. Hold the position for a count of five, breathing normally. Inhale and return to an upright position. Hold for five with your arms still high, then relax your arms. You should experience a lovely warm glow as the shoulder and neck muscles relax. Repeat three times.

FACIAL YOGA

Who needs a Botox party when you can look daft and have a laugh at the same time? When you think about it, your face works darn hard all day long. It chews, speaks, laughs, cries, kisses, grimaces, frowns and sneezes. And, like your body, facial muscles soak up and store a lot of stress and tension, all of which reflect in your face. To stop you auditioning for a lookalike of the wicked witch in panto, give your face a workout and give your girlfriends a laugh by doing the following facial exercises. They will relax tense muscles and improve blood flow to the skin and tissues.

Clenched smile

Grit your teeth (like the time when your boyfriend gave you one day's notice he was off on a lad's holiday for a week) and open your lips as wide as they will go. Feel your lips, cheeks, chin and neck stretch to their limit. Hold and release. Repeat.

Scrunchies

Scrunch and screw your face up very tightly. Purse your lips, draw your cheeks in towards your nose, pull your eyebrows down and bring the flesh of your chin up towards your mouth. Hold and release.

The lion

Take a deep breath, then breathe out forcefully while opening your mouth wide and sticking out your tongue as far as it will go. Then (this is the fun bit), growl as loud as you can, open your eyes and look up. This is a great way to remove tension in the jaw.

Cheek pinching

Pinch your cheeks by grabbing small bits of flesh and giving them a gentle squeeze.

Super-easy massage

Anybody can massage. There's no great master plan; all you need is a pair of sensitive hands and the desire to make your friends feel good. Massage is the ultimate treatment to help you unwind, lift your spirits and increase blood supply to the tissues for improved muscle tone. Literally just go with the flow and be led by your hands. Practise the following basic routines (you can vary them as you want) on your friends and then swap around.

SOOTHING STROKES ... AND WHAT THEY MEAN

Massage invariably comes naturally, and once you've got to grips with it you can experiment and vary your touch. A brisk hand is invigorating, whereas slow and tender moves are more peaceful. Here are a few moves you can try:

- **Basic effleurage** Hands are laid flat on the part of the body to be treated. Fingers should mould themselves to the contours of the body using firm and soothing motions. Pressure should be applied when working towards the heart and gently released on the return.
- **Petrissage** Taking hold of the edge of a muscle, or part of the muscle that lies close to the bone and squeezing it with fingertips and thumbs.
- **Circular** Ideal for legs and back. The hands move firmly up and around the area one at a time, forming large circles that should cover the whole area.
- **Figure of eight** This is one of the best movements to give and receive and is great for soothing away tension in the back. It's a powerful move and, if done correctly, deeply relaxing. Both hands work at the same time but in opposite directions, each forming a figure of eight on the area.
- **Kneading** Best used on fleshy areas such as the tops of the arms and thighs. The action will improve circulation.
- **Feather stroking** Used as a finishing-off technique. The fingertips are used to calm nerve endings, and one hand gently follows the other. The movements should get lighter and lighter until they are no more than a featherlight stroke.

SMOOTH MOVES FOR NECK AND FACE

1. Stand behind your friend and effleurage from the sides of the head, down the neck, over the shoulders to the upper arms. Repeat six times.

2. Petrissage the ridge of the shoulders. Use your thumbs and rest the fingers over the shoulders, moving from the centre to the outside edges for 20 seconds.

3. Hold the forehead in the palm of your right hand and petrissage by lightly squeezing up and down the back of the neck for 20 seconds. Repeat on the other side.

4. Rest the back of the head against your tummy and effleurage from the forehead to the temples and from the chin to the temple six times. Petrissage for 20 seconds using the fingertips to circle lightly over the face.

5. Use tapping motions with fingertips one after the other and drum lightly all over the face. Avoid the eyes and the tip of the nose.

6. Supporting the head with one hand, effleurage one side from the head through the neck and shoulders to the upper arms six times. Repeat on the other side.

A BRISK RUB FOR UPTIGHT SHOULDERS

1. Start with soothing effleurage strokes around the shoulder blades.
2. Using the thumbs, make alternate strokes to the left-hand side of the neck and right up into the hairline. Swap to the other side.
3. Pick up, squeeze and release the shoulder muscles from the shoulder edge along to the neck.

THE BEST EVER HAND MASSAGE

It's surprising how much tension a hand holds. This quick massage is ultra-simple but very effective in loosening up palms and joints.

1. Using a good base oil, such as sweet almond, pour roughly ½ teaspoon of oil onto the palm of your hand, then rub the oil over both your palms.
2. Gently spread the oil around your friend's hand using light, stroking movements.
3. Move your thumbs away from each other from the centre of the hand towards the outsides. Do this a couple of times.
4. Now move your thumbs between the tendons of the back of the hand, pushing up towards the

wrist. You can also try small circular movements between the tendons, too. Repeat a couple of times.

5. Take each finger in turn between your own finger and thumb and make small twisting or circular movements up and down each finger, finishing with their thumb.

6. Flip the hand over and move your thumbs away from each other. From the centre of the palm press more firmly with your own thumbs.

7. Make small circular movements with your thumbs all over the palm.

8. Finish by cupping the hand. Now do the same for the other hand.

... THEN ONTO THE ARMS

1. Hold the hand and effleurage the arm six times. Place the flexed arm on a pillow.

2. Rest your friend's hand against your tummy and massage the forearm by stroking from the wrist to the elbow six times.

3. Petrissage the lower arm softly, squeezing up and down the forearm for 30 seconds.

4. Effleurage deeply from wrist to elbow six times. Steady the forearm and lead with your thumbs, down the centre and to each side.

5. Extend the arm, placing it between your arm and chest. Massage from elbow to shoulder six times.

PARTY POOPER A cold room. It makes the muscles contract and you won't feel relaxed.

PARTY SOOTHER Making sure the room is warm will make you 'open' to the massage.

Essential oil know-how

As it would be unthinkable for any fully signed up I-want-to-look-my-most-fabulous girl not to condition her hair after shampooing, it would also be a beauty sin not to massage skin with a good quality essential oil. Using oils on your skin can produce amazing results. They are easily absorbed and take ingredients deeper into the skin than the most expensive of creams. Not only do oils smooth the skin and give a touch of luxury but they also help hands glide better. Using an oil will help your hands develop a fluid motion with no friction. **Warning:** Essential oils should never be used undiluted and some should be avoided during pregnancy or by those with asthma or epilepsy.

The essential-oil lowdown

Basil Soothing and uplifting
Camomile Relaxing, soothes aches and pains
Clary sage Invigorating and uplifting
Frankincense Rejuvenating and soothing
Geranium Puts you in a good mood
Grapefruit Detoxifying and purifying
Jasmine Exotic and soothing
Juniper Boosts energy and beats stress
Lavender Calming and restoring
Lemon Wakes up the mind
Neroli Good for tension and anxiety
Patchouli Anti-inflammatory and grounding
Peppermint Warms and refreshes
Rosemary Energising and clears the head
Sandalwood Deeply soothing

IN THE MIX

To blend your own girlie aromatherapy treat all you need to do is add drops of essential oil to a good quality carrier oil such as sweet almond or wheatgerm oil – the latter is a more nourishing choice for winter as it helps hydrate dry skin. As a general guideline blend between 10-12 drops of essential oil into 30 ml/

2 tablespoons carrier massage oil. The trick is to choose an essential oil that will reflect or enhance your mood. Unless you're a fully trained therapist don't use essential oils on a pregnant friend – just stick to the carrier oil.

DIY BLISSED-OUT BLENDS

Half the fun of giving a massage is mixing up your own blends. Here are a couple of recipes to enhance your soothing strokes as well as perfuming the room.

BE-KIND-TO-ME BLEND
To 30 ml/2 tablespoons of sweet almond oil add:
4 drops sandalwood essential oil
4 drops patchouli essential oil
2 drops basil essential oil

PEP-ME-UP BLEND
To 30 ml/2 tablespoons of sweet almond oil add:
4 drops grapefruit essential oil
4 drops peppermint essential oil
2 drops rosemary essential oil

MAKE-ME-BEAUTIFUL SKIN SAUNAS
This steamy ritual will open pores and prepare your complexion for a face mask – more of which later.

Fill a bowl with almost boiling water and add 4 drops of each of the following:

For normal skin, mandarin and lavender
For oily skin, lemon and eucalyptus
For dry skin, rose and camomile.

Hold your face above the bowl, but distance it about 30cm/12in from the steam for 2 minutes.

PARTY POOPER Brushing the oil directly onto the body like you're basting a turkey.

PARTY SOOTHER Pouring oil into the palms of your hands to warm the oil before soothing it onto the body.

Alternative therapies

Here are a few more of the therapies that have become popular in the last few years.

THE DIY INDIAN HEAD MASSAGE

OK girls, this is the perfect treatment for a night in, as you will be leaving the party with oily hair – not such a good look when trying to impress in the outside world! Indian head massage is as common as cleaning your teeth in India. The different movements can ease tension as well as promote strong, healthy hair, plus it's deeply relaxing. I've had a couple and literally nodded off. Although you can do it on yourself, it's more beneficial when you buddy up and have it done for you. Here's how to do it:

1. Rub a dessertspoon of oil (a base oil is good enough) into your hands and stroke it evenly all over the scalp. Smooth it evenly over the scalp from front to back.
2. Cradle the head between your hands and, with the heels of your hands resting on the temples, let your fingers meet at the top of the head.
3. Now exert as much pressure as is comfortable. If your girlfriend yelps you know it's too much. Hold the head for a minute. Move your hands a little further back and repeat this head hold.
4. Next, the scalp lift. Interlock your fingers and slowly press the palms of your hands inwards and upwards against the scalp. Feel the scalp move between your fingers.
5. Finish off by using your finger pads (not tips) on the points in the middle of the top of the head halfway between the ears, as this is the most

powerful sedative point in the body and helps balance emotions. If the scalp feels as tight as a drum that means there's a lot of tension. Continue working on this area until the scalp starts to loosen.

Reflexology

Look further than pedicures and Jimmy Choo's when talking feet, as reflexology can come to the rescue of the emotionally walking wounded! Your feet mirror your body, and by stimulating specific reflex points on them you can restore the body's equilibrium and encourage the release of toxins. The great thing about reflexology is that you can DIY it. The only technique to master is 'thumb walking'. This is where you use tiny caterpillar-like movements to inch your way along the foot. The ideal time to do reflexology is when feet are bare and you're relaxed – so the UGNI is just the occasion!

Now, if you're foot happy you can offer to be a DIY reflexologist to one of your girlfriends. If you're not too ticklish you can offer your feet back for her to work on, otherwise just stick to doing your own feet. In reflexology massage, the thumb or the entire knuckle is used in a deep, rotating motion. Start at the heel of the foot, which corresponds to the lower part of the body such as the sciatic nerve, and then move up to the toes, which are linked to the head. Take note of the reflex zones reflected on your feet shown in the diagram below and let your thumbs do the walking.

DR FEET'S WELL-BEING ZONES

A quick way of getting your head around the practice of reflexology is to divide your feet up into four sections, as shown on the chart. The top section, including the toe, relates to the head area; the upper section of the feet (just below the ball of the big toe), to the chest area; the middle section of the feet relates to the abdominal organs; and the heel area to the pelvic organs. Here's a guide to the benefits of working each area.

- **Brain** Improves circulation and helps relieve headaches.
- **Colon** Helps to eliminate waste products, relieves gas and blocked bowels.
- **Ears** Opens passageways. Great to do after a flight.
- **Eyes** Work on this area to help combat puffiness around the eyes.
- **Heart** Improves blood circulation for all over well-being.

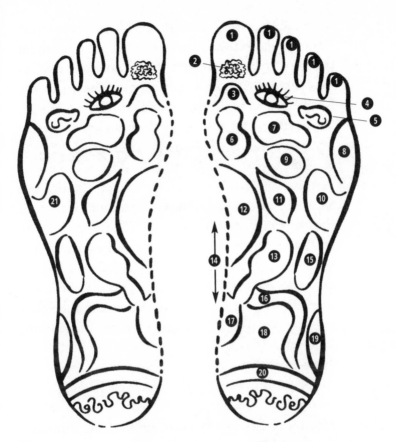

1. sinus
2. brain
3. neck
4. eye
5. ear
6. thyroid
7. lung
8. shoulder
9. solar plexus
10. heart
11. thymus
12. stomach
13. kidney
14. spine
15. spleen
16. colon
17. bladder
18. small intestine
19. hip
20. sciatic nerve
21. liver

- **Kidneys** Detoxifies and prevents bloating by ridding toxins. Good for acne.
- **Liver** Filters blood and aids fat digestion.
- **Lung** Strengthens the respiratory system.
- **Neck** Relaxes and loosen the muscles.
- **Sciatic nerve** Helps relieve pain from the nerve that runs from the base of the heel up to the butt.
- **Shoulder** Helps with shoulders riding as high as earrings.
- **Sinus** Clears congested sinuses to make you breathe more effortlessly.
- **Small Intestine** Improves absorption of vital nutrients.
- **Solar Plexus** Referred to as the 'nerve switch-board' of the body, as it's the main storage for stress. Press your thumb into the spot and hold for a few seconds to help balance the nervous system and Zen you out.
- **Spine** Improves circulation and rids the spine of stiffness. Thumb-walk your way up the length of your foot.
- **Spleen** Purifies and balances iron deficiencies.
- **Stomach** Improves tummy troubles such as indigestion and bloating.
- **Thymus** Energises. Press for two minutes to ease stress.
- **Thyroid** Regulates the metabolism and revs up sex drive!

Mystic hand signals

....

We all love a Gypsy Rose Lee in our life – a woman who's swathed in fringed shawls, wears large gold hoop earrings and stares intently into our palms. After crossing her palm with silver she reveals you are going to meet a tall, dark, handsome man, make lots of money and be happy ever after. Yeah, right! But why not add a bit of mystic magic into your UGNI where you can have fun with hand reading? This isn't fortune telling, but more about personality, revealing how you can 'read' your girlfriend's hidden depths and traits by the shape of her fingers, nails and hands. Alternatively, why not put the test to your boyfriend's hand shape and then work out if you should keep him or dump him!

FINGER POINTING

Finger type Pointed and delicate with long fingers
Personality Sensitive, mysterious and idealistic. If a girl, think Phoebe in *Friends*.

Finger type Knobbly fingers with large knuckle bones
Personality Interested in theories and mind-orientated activities (in other words, the brainy one). They are logical with good judgment.

Finger type Squarish fingers
Personality Lives life by the rules with an honest approach to everything they do. Can be self-assured and stubborn.

Finger type Rounded fingers
Personality Active is their second name, and they enjoy sports and the outdoor life. Also loves animals.

Finger type Short, blunt fingers
Personality Careless, impulsive and often unpredictable. A night with them is always fun – and sometimes dangerous!

What your nail shape reveals
Nail shape Short
Personality Has energy, is curious and shows great intuition.

Nail shape Broad
Personality Shows good judgment and clarity of thought.

Nail shape Long
Personality Easy going. Little ruffles their feathers.

Finger type Smooth and tapered fingers
Personality Artistic, sensitive and creative. Good motivators but can be hypercritical of others.

The four basic hand shapes (...and how to read them):

Square
Description The palm is as wide as it's long. The fingers will be squared at the ends and the hand will show few lines.
Personality Down-to-earth and reliable. This person is a hard worker with a responsible attitude.
Faults As the name suggests, can be a little bit square! They are often resistant to change, so need livening up.

Conic
Description The fingers are tapered and rounded, and the hand has a rounded base. The thumb often bends outwards.
Personality Loves art and beauty. They enjoy entertaining and often make good hostesses! They are quick to learn, gossip like crazy and are very likeable. However, they can be manipulative if the mood takes them.
Faults Can have a tendency to be superficial. So expect lots of air kissing darhling!

Pointed

Description Delicate with graceful hands and long, pointed fingers.

Personality Often called the 'psychic' as they have great interest in psychic matters. They have strong intuition and often 'know' what others are thinking. They love anything to do with showbusiness.

Faults Can live in a world of fantasy where facing up to hard truths upsets them.

Spatulate

Description This hand has a narrow base that broadens towards the tip. The fingers are broad and spade shaped at the tips.

Personality A real individual. They are creative, but still practical, and love activity and travel. They're great company with plenty of va-va-voom.

Faults Can be an unstable and unreliable girlfriend (for men).

CHAPTER 7

The pleasure of pampering

A perfect pedicure, heavenly hands, soft-to-the-touch skin and a radiant complexion are all beauty wishes we would love to be granted. And they can be with the UGNI. More of us girls are beginning to understand the true value of pampering time. And the experts also agree that the pay-off for truly indulging your beauty pleasures is a happier woman. Yes, when you look great you automatically feel more powerful, more in control and therefore happy, happy, happy. If you love the colour of your new nails, or the results of a facial mask you've whipped up along with your girlfriends, then it will have a beneficial effect on your mind and body chemistry. It's where beauty and medicine merge. So with these facts in your mind there's never been a better reason to set up your very own home spa – just treat it as a one-night vacation! The secret is to reclaim run-of-the-mill beauty rituals and make them experiences to share and enjoy for one indulgent night.

Benefits of a home spa

- You don't have to make an appointment.
- You don't have to worry about looking like your nan in public (all hair nets and cold creams).
- You don't have to leave a tip.
- You don't have to worry about going home with greasy hair.
- You can keep your pants on.

Welcome to my spa world

Stepping into a swish day spa makes us feel special and 'worth it', so to make your girlfriends feel they've stepped into a temple of cocooning delight in your own home when throwing a Pampering To Go night, it's important to get the atmosphere exactly right. Greeting your girls at the door with a cigarette between your lips and munching from a packet of crisps doesn't create the impression that you are the madam of their luxury me-time. To escape life's stresses and strains you want to create a home that feels like The Great Escape – all candles and fluffy white towels, not porridge and prison bars! Here are a few tips on creating a heavenly home haven:

- Light scented candles or burn aromatherapy oils to instil an aura of relative calm. A nice idea is to scent a light bulb: shake out a couple of drops of essential oil onto a tissue and wipe onto the bulb. The heat from the bulb will then flood the room with a not too overpowering scent.
- Big, fluffy towels are essential. Ask each of your spa-ing girlfriends to bring over a couple of their own with their own pedicure and manicure must-haves (see the checklist further down).
- Ask everybody to kick off their shoes the minute

they enter your 'spa' and supply them with flip-flops. (Buy up cheap ones from Woolworth's.)

- Tidy up as much as possible. I know I've mentioned this at the beginning of the book, but I can't overemphasise it for your pampering pleasure. Too much clutter doesn't make guests feel calm; it makes them feel chaotic.

- Play soothing music. I'm not talking soundtracks of dolphins, whales, tropical birds or sounds of the sea (they are enough to drive a girl nuts) but grooves from a chill-out album. Buy a couple and play all evening.

- Offer up a cup of green tea as their aperitif. All the best spas have it as their 'tipple' and it's full of antioxidants to ward off all those nasty free radicals the girls encountered on getting to your house. They can go on to cocktails later on in the evening.

- Make sure the bathroom is clean. Yes, again mentioned, but for a pampering evening the bathroom will become the main focus.

First steps: let's talk feet

Hardly anybody thinks of their feet as sexy, but believe me the foot and leg hold many hidden messages! First off, the science bit: in neural biology the brain has a map linking one part of the body to another – the feet go with the genitals which may go a long way to explaining why your boyfriend has a fascination for your stilettos! And secondly, feet talk. Oh yes, they do! Do the feet-talking test with your girlfriends before kicking off with the serious pampering stuff of pedicuring.

WHAT ARE YOUR FEET SAYING?

Action Foot tapping.
You're saying I'm bored.

Action Feet pointing towards a person you're talking with.
You're saying I'm enjoying you and what you're saying.

Action One foot placed on top of the other.
You're saying I'm not too sure about you.

Action Placing your foot on an object such as a table or car bumper.

You're saying I'm in charge here, buster!

Action When sitting in a chair, feet planted back from the knees and crossed at the ankles.
You're saying I'm acting proper and I'm a little bit shy.

Action Feet placed wide apart and flat on the ground.
You're saying I'm strong and powerful. Don't mess with me!

PLAYING FOOTSIE: WHAT KIND OF LOVER ARE YOU?

Walking style Slow and plodding. Feet firmly on the ground, slowly placing one foot in front of the other.
Sex style You're an earthy lover. You're loyal, but could do with getting out of a sexual rut.

Walking style A quick stepper where feet hardly touch the ground.
Sex style You're easily excitable, passionate and a little hard to control!

Walking style A bouncer and often walks on tiptoe.
Sex style You love variety in a lover and like to try out lots of different things. You get bored easily.

Walking style Slow but light.
Sex style Deeply emotional and intense.

HOW TO DO PERFECT FEET
(IT'S CALLED FANCY FOOTWORK)

Now we've established that feet are sexy and they can actually talk, how about looking after them a little more beyond the odd slap and tickle with a squirt of foot lotion and a sweep of nail polish? Getting to the sole of the matter, you and your girls can perk up aching feet with exercises, and when performed regularly these will tone up weakened muscles and strengthen the arches, thereby helping to ward off the cramping effects of high-heeled shoes.

A workout for feet

- **Walking on the outer edges of the feet** This relieves the strain on the muscles of the inner arch and helps tone up the contracted muscles of the outer arch.
- **Rising on tiptoes** Stand with feet parallel and rise slowly up and down ten times. This exercises the leg muscles and helps strengthens the foot muscles.
- **Bending toes downwards** Stand on a telephone directory with toes projecting over the edge. Bend them downwards as far as possible. Although

this may be uncomfortable at first, take note that it helps strengthen and tone up the muscles in front of the foot.

- **Rotate the feet** Extend the feet one at a time and rotate slowly at the ankle as if trying to draw a large circle with the big toe. Repeat in the opposite direction.

- **Extending the sole of the foot** Extend and stretch the foot, trying to keep it in a straight line with the leg.

- **Tennis ball rolling** Roll a tennis ball back and forth under your foot. It helps rebalance foot muscles that have become stiff from wearing heels.

READY-TO-WEAR FEET (THE SPA-WORTHY HOME PEDICURE)

Checklist:

nail polish remover	tissues
large bowl or foot spa	pumice stone or foot file
milk bath	toenail clippers
exfoliator	nail file
cuticle oil	nail polish
orangewood stick	base and topcoats
cotton wool	toe separators
foot cream	

1. Remove any polish from the toenails and then create a spa-like foot soak by filling a bowl half-full of warm water. (If you have a foot spa, then so much the better.) Add a capful of milk bath for a hydrating soak. Soak feet for 15 minutes to cleanse the foot and soften hard skin; it will also relax the whole body from the tip of your toes to the top of your head.

2. To loosen dead skin and help circulation, massage feet with an exfoliating foot scrub.

3. Take feet out and dry off well, especially in between the toes. Apply cuticle oil to the base of each nail, leave to soak for a few minutes then gently push down the cuticles using an orange-wood stick. Twirl a little cotton wool around the end so as not to dig and prod the cuticle. Wipe the nail bed clean with a tissue.

4. Using a pumice stone or foot file, attack any areas of rough skin.

5. Next, use toenail clippers to cut the nails in a straight line, then file gently in one direction. Your toenails should be kept short and square. Leaving the nails too long or over-filing at the sides can cause ingrowing toenails and possibly infection.

6. Using a foot lotion give the feet a massage (see box for the best-ever foot massage).

7. Wipe off any residue from the lotion, especially

on the nails, otherwise the polish won't glide on, and begin by applying a base coat. (This acts as double-sided tape, as it sticks to the nail and to the polish.) Use toe separators to make the polishing job easier.

8. Apply two coats of your favourite nail colour – slowly. A hurried paint job looks just that! For emergencies have to hand a cotton-wool-covered orange stick soaked in nail polish remover to tidy up any slip-ups.

9. Finally, seal the colour with a topcoat. Avoid wearing shoes for two hours.

THE BEST-EVER FOOT MASSAGE

Do this alone or partner up with a (willing) girlfriend:

1. Using a base massage oil blend with cypress, peppermint and rosemary essential oils for the ultimate wake-up-pooped-feet foot remedy.

2. Start with the inner arches of the foot (the raised part in the area underneath). Using both hands, gently stroke up towards the toes using your thumbs. Slowly increase the pressure.

3. Next, focus on the ball of the foot, applying pressure with your thumb in small circular motions. This can be a very sensitive area so don't overdo

it on someone else. If they shout 'Stop!' stop.

4. Now gently rotate each toe, pulling each one by placing a finger and thumb on either side and sliding firmly from the base to the tip of the toe.
5. Working down from the ankle, massage firmly between the bones with thumbs and fingers.
6. Hold the ankle and, with your other hand, run strong, long strokes from the back of the knee to the ankle.
7. Finish by rotating the ankle and gently stroking the feet all over. Cup the feet between the palms of your hands to finish the massage ritual.

THE BEST-EVER FOOT MASK

A paraffin foot mask is an all-round cosseting mask that you will find in the best spas worldwide – which, incidentally, you will pay top dollar for. It acts as a full-on rescue treatment for the most downtrodden of feet. Take note that it can also be used on hands, too.

1. Melt four bars of paraffin wax (available at hardware stores) in a microwave in a bowl. If you don't have a microwave, melt in an old bowl inside a pan of gently simmering water.
2. Massage the feet with a rich moisturiser.
3. Test the temperature of the wax first with your

little finger. Then dip the feet into the warm paraffin wax three times, allowing them to dry in between each layer of wax.

4. Wrap each foot with clingfilm tightly enough to make an airtight seal. This helps moisture to penetrate the skin.
5. Leave for 20 minutes to set.
6. Remove the wrap and peel off the wax.
7. Gasp at and stroke your ultra-smooth feet.

PARTY POOPER Having a room full of smelly socks. Chuck all your guests' socks into a pillowcase.

PARTY SOOTHER Using cushions and pillows as footrests after treatments.

Nailing the flawless manicure

Spa etiquette dictates that nails should always be perfectly buffed, filed and polished as there's nothing more pleasing than a perfect set of ten. Do-it-yourself manicures, like pedicures, can be as professional-looking as those done by a manicurist; the secret is taking your time. This is why manicures are a perfect treat for the UGNI.

A CLASSIC MANICURE

Checklist:

cotton pad
nail polish remover
cotton wool
orangewood stick
emery board
cuticle remover
nail polish

bowl
exfoliator
nail brush
base and topcoats
whitening toothpaste
  (if necessary)

1. Remove any old nail polish with a cotton pad soaked with nail polish remover. Repeat until all polish has gone. Remove any stubborn polish around the cuticles with a cotton-wool-covered cuticle stick dipped in remover.
2. Shape your nails using an emery board, filing nails

until the corners are slightly rounded. This is known as a 'squoval' in manicure speak. Stroke from the edges of the nail towards the centre. Do not saw the nails; this can cause tears.

3. Apply cuticle remover around the contour area, then soak your fingertips in a small bowl filled with warm water for a couple of minutes. Gently roll back the cuticles with a cuticle stick wrapped in cotton wool, working away the dead tissue to form a neat outline.

4. Get a girlfriend to treat you to a hand massage (see page 132).

5. Wash hands thoroughly. You can use a scrub for the back of the hands at this point, too. If nails are yellow use whitening toothpaste to brighten them up. Scrub nails with a slightly abrasive paste to take away any stains. The secret of a long-lasting manicure is that the nail plate must be squeaky clean before base coat and topcoat are applied.

6. Brush on a base coat and let it dry for a few minutes.

7. Roll your chosen nail colour between the palms of your hands before using and apply in two thin coats. Starting with your pinkie, place the first brush stroke down the centre of the nail, then fill in the sides. Continue with the other nails. Wait a couple of minutes and apply a second coat.

8. Finish with a clear topcoat and let the nails dry for at least 30 minutes.

Facing up to skin solutions

Just think of this section as your one-night stand to a gorgeous complexion. There's little doubt that a supercharged facial is the starting point for fresh and healthy-looking skin. Cleansing, toning and hiding behind a mask guarantees to give you that lit-from-within skin that spas specialise in. And with a few insider secrets at your fingertips, too, such as making up your own face masks from kitchen-cupboard ingredients, you can be sure you'll walk away from your evening looking radiant, not ravaged! So, for one night only, girls, it's time to drop the soap-and-water act and offer up your pores for a luxury DIY facial.

READ YOUR FACE

Your health is written all over your face, so become a DIY skin therapist and read each other's skin to throw up clues about how to handle your lifestyle for better-looking skin.

Forehead Traditionally, this area is regarded as the 'sister'

161

to the bladder and the digestive system. If you suffer from breakouts frequently here it might mean that you need to improve your elimination. In other words drink more water (yes, that again) and eat more 'whole' foods such as wholemeal bread, nuts, pulses, and vegetables and fruits complete with skins on.

Middle of the forehead This area is related to the liver. Congestion in this zone can point to an over-zealous appetite for alcohol and rich foods. Ease off if you want to blast the zits.

Ears Yes, they are classified as part of your face! Ears are related to the kidneys, so if you notice that your ears are very hot, it's not that someone is talking about you, but you're stressing them out with stimulants. Cut down on the alcohol and caffeine.

Cheeks Smokers can suffer from fine and broken capillaries in this area, as the cheeks relate to the lungs. The answer? Cut down and then quit if you're serious about saving your skin.

Under eyes Dark circles here indicate that you are dehydrated. Drink – yes, you've guessed it – more water.

Chin Breakouts or hair growth can point to a hormonal

imbalance, or full-on stress. Premenstrual breakouts are also very common in this area, too. If blemishes persist see your doctor, as you may need prescribed help.

PARTY POOPER Making your friend feel bad about her skin.

PARTY SOOTHER Making your friend feel good about her skin. Always point out the positives before the negatives. A good facialist will always do this.

THE FABULISING FACIALS

Although a spa will offer a menu of facials, each with I-don't-believe-it names such as 'never have a blackhead again' facial or 'zap your wrinkles forever' facial, you only need to cut through the clever marketing and let your common sense tell you that electric prods waved over the face and oxygen blasted into your pores won't leave you with a skin as smooth and flawless as alabaster. Essentially every facial minus the gimmicks includes the basics of: cleansing, massage, extraction, mask and moisturising, and that's what I believe gets results. Here's the professional way of doing it:

Checklist:
shower cap
cleanser
good quality cotton wool pads (preferably ones that are
   non-scratchy; for this reason don't use tissues)
toner
exfoliator
clean cloth
essential oils (optional)
tissues
tea tree oil
magnifying mirror (so that you can see your skin in
   great detail, including blackheads)
face mask
moisturiser

1. Tie your hair back and wash your hands. Dirty
    hands on the face are not a good start. Put on a
    shower cap (this not only protects the hair, but
    also encourages you to deep cleanse and pay
    attention to the sides of the face and the ears).
2. Deep cleanse by warming your cleanser between
    the palms of your hands before massaging it over
    your face. Not only does this help emulsify the
    cream but also the heat from your fingertips
    makes it more effective in loosening grime. This
    helps soften any congested areas in the skin and

relaxes the pores for further treatment. For this reason spend longer than you usually would working the cleanser in.

3. Remove the cleanser with damp cotton wool pads.

4. Swipe over a toner that doesn't contain alcohol. An alcoholic cleanser will tighten the pores before the treatment is finished.

5. Use an exfoliator to slough off dead skin cells and give skin a childlike brightness. Massage over the face gently using your finger pads (not tips). Do not over-scrub, as this will leave the skin looking red and feeling irritated. Rinse thoroughly with warm water and a clean cloth.

6. Steam the face to perk up a sluggish complexion. Half fill a glass bowl with boiling water. Allow to cool slightly to avoid burning the face, then cover the head and bowl with a towel to lock in the steam. Use some of the essential oil suggestions in The Make-Me-Beautiful Skin Saunas on page 136.

7. Extract if need be. Now, this isn't a licence to go popping lots of blackheads and whiteheads reck-lessly; there's an art to it. Firstly wrap your two index fingers in tissue that has been dipped into tea tree oil, then apply firm pressure around the offending blemish to push it out of the pore. Do not dig or force it. Extractions can be uncomfort-able, but they should not leave red, swollen marks.

8. Spread a mask onto your face generously (see the recipes below). Leave for 10–15 minutes.
9. Remove and rinse thoroughly.
10. Smooth on a soothing moisturiser.

Your fingertips: the best anti-ageing tools

Spending time massaging in a good moisturising cream will increase micro-circulation to the top layers of the skin. This results in the delivery of much-needed nutrients and oxygen to the skin and the draining away of toxins. Touch softens the skin; in essence it brings back that sought-after glow. Follow these moves for complexion perfection:

THE YOUTH-REVIVING FACIAL MASSAGE

This is a nice massage to have done to you as it's best received when lying down.

1. Use firm pressure to massage in small circles along the brow bone. This helps stimulate key pressure points that will help drain away toxins from your eyes and out into your sinuses.

2. Gently massage the eye socket by following the curve of your eyeball.
3. Finish by pulsing two fingers beneath your eyes, working on the area where your cheeks join your nose to reduce under-eye puffiness.

THE PARTY-GIRL FACIAL MASSAGE

Alcohol is the curse of great-looking skin, as it hangs onto toxins and leads to bloating. This massage helps drain toxins.

1. Leaning on a hard surface, take the full weight of your face in your hands, then massage upwards and outwards with fingers using large strokes.
2. Hook the heels of your hands under your jaw line and drop your face forward, placing your little finger alongside your nose. Massage from the centre outwards in a wavelike motion. This will help sculpt your cheekbones.
3. Stroke downwards from the temples to the neck, draining fluid down and away from your face.

THE GLOW-GIVER FACIAL MASSAGE

Put the flush back into your complexion with moves that rejuvenate.

1. Press a warm towel onto your face. This will cause a rush of blood to the skin's surface and boost circulation.
2. Gently use your fingertips to crawl over your cheeks, nipping the skin very softly.
3. Pinch your cheeks between your thumbs and forefingers and roll the skin back and forth.

Facial oils ... pick your slick

As mentioned, oils married with massage makes for a great treatment; just make sure you use the right oil for your skin type.

- **Vitamin E oil** Rich in antioxidants and great for very dry skin.
- **Grapeseed oil** Again, rich in antioxidants and suitable for oily to combination skin, thanks to its light texture.
- **Jojoba oil** Classed as a balancing oil and good for troubled skin (acne, psoriasis and eczema).

Kitchen-cupboard beautifying secrets

....

Bring some Eastern spice (and I'm talking more than a takeaway curry) to your girls' night in with Indian-inspired beauty treatments. Yes, forget the Hollywood makeover, it's all about the Bollywood makeover.

Spas know more than anybody else that Indian culture is privy to ancient and natural beauty remedies that have been passed down from generation to generation. And the best thing of all is that they're cheap as well as being effective. Simple and beautifying ingredients can be found not in an overpriced pharmacy or department store but in grocery and health-food shops.

For example, in some cases pimples can simply be cleared up with a pinch of spice available from Asian supermarkets. The power of turmeric is renowned in India as an effective spot treatment. Simply take 1 teaspoon of it along with a pinch of fine sea salt (a neutraliser of bacteria) and 2 teaspoons of honey (soothing). Mix it up into a thick paste, pick it up with a cotton bud and dab onto the offending spot.

THE BRIDAL MASK
This is the traditional Indian mask used by a bride seven days before her marriage.

You will need
50 g/1³/₄ oz/¹/₂ cup gram flour (available from health shops)
2 teaspoons ground turmeric
2 teaspoons of sandalwood powder
2 teaspoons almond oil

Superskin shake-up
1 *Mix the ingredients in a bowl and add a little water to make a smooth paste.*

2 *Apply to the face and leave for up to 10 minutes. Rub with the palms and fingers to remove all the paste. Rinse and moisturise.*

YOGURT AND ZESTY LEMON FACE MASK
Great for an overtired skin, as the egg white acts as a skin tightener.

You will need
¹/₂ teaspoon honey
juice of ¹/₂ lemon
3 tablespoons yogurt
1 egg white

Superskin shake-up

1 *Mix all the ingredients together. Beat the egg white until soft peaks form and then stir into the honey and yogurt mixture.*

2 *Apply to the face and leave for about 15 minutes. Wash off with warm water.*

APPLE ZINGER FACE MASK
Honey is gentle and moisturising for the skin and apple is a useful exfoliator.

You will need
1 medium-sized apple, finely grated
5 tablespoons honey

Superskin shake-up
1 *Mix the apple and honey together.*

2 *Smooth over the skin and leave for 10 minutes. Wash off with warm water.*

EGG AND HONEY FACE MASK
An easy mask for all skin types. Egg yolks contain antioxidants, which are classed as skin heroes.

You will need
1 egg yolk
1 teaspoon honey
1 teaspoon vitamin E oil
1 teaspoon almond oil

Superskin shake-up

1 *Mix all the ingredients together, stirring until smooth.*

2 *Apply to the face and leave for 15 minutes. Rinse off with warm water.*

PAPAYA AND CLAY GLOWING FACE MASK
The natural enzymes in the papaya will help dissolve dead skin cells while the clay is helpful for oily skin.

You will need
1 tablespoon fuller's earth
1 tablespoon honey
1 tablespoon mashed papaya

Superskin shake-up

1 *Mix the ingredients together until well blended.*

2 *Smooth on the face and leave for 20 minutes. Rinse off with warm water.*

ROSE PETAL RELAXING CLEANSER
A fragrant and cleansing wash that leaves the face looking relaxed. Watch a person smell a rose and see what I mean!

You will need
1½ cups full-cream milk
30 ml/1 fl oz/2 tbsp vegetable glycerine
1 cup rose petals (freshly picked and clean)

Superskin shake-up

1 *Fill a pan with water and place a heatproof bowl on top (like a double boiler). Heat until the water begins to simmer in the pan and then pour the milk into the bowl above.*

2 *Add the vegetable glycerine and rose petals (picked from the garden or bought from a florist, or insist your boyfriend Interfloras you some). Remove from the heat and let the mixture cool. Once the mixture is cool to the touch, pour into a blender and mix well.*

3 *Wash your face with the mixture and rinse with warm water. (This mixture can be refrigerated for up to 4 days.)*

THE LITTLE EXTRAS

DARK CIRCLE LIGHTENER
Wrap a grated raw potato in cheesecloth and apply to the under-eye area for 15 minutes.

LUSCIOUS LIP POTION
Grate raw coconut and squeeze out the milk. Rub the milk over the lips.

Fruity beauty

Cherry-pick your favourite ingredients and whizz up your own personal recipes to apply to your face and neck and even to your body for nourishment and to deep-clean pores. Here's the lowdown on fruity beauty:

- **Apple** contains malic acid, a powerful exfoliator for the skin.
- **Banana** is moisturising and filled with potassium, which is essential for healthy skin.
- **Cucumber** Cooling, astringent and depuffing.
- **Ginger** warms up the body something wonderful. Good for poor circulation or those who suffer from cold feet (hopefully not the bride-to-be!).
- **Honey** attracts and keeps in moisture. A brilliant anti-irritant, so great for touchy skins.
- **Lemon** A natural purifier, astringent and cleanser. Perfect for oily skins.
- **Lime** cleanses and purifies the skin as well as smelling great.
- **Melon** A skin soother brimming with antioxidants and vitamins.
- **Orange** An astringent with anti-inflammatory qualities.
- **Papaya** contains enzymes that help dissolve and lift dead skin cells. Great to use in a mask.

- **Pineapple** A gentle and natural exfoliator.
- **Sea salt** A quick-fix all-over-body exfoliator. Mineralises the skin, helping it towards radiance and softness.
- **Strawberry** Contains fruit enzymes that help soften the skin.
- **Yogurt** A super-soothing cleanser, moisturiser and anti-inflammatory.

Top spa secrets

Any spa worth its salt scrub has its own special rituals, which is one of the reasons why girls flock to them like bees to a honey pot. These special rituals give the desired results of making you feel extra special. Here are a few your friends can take away from your evening and then try at home:

- **No shoes, no news:** A policy at many spas where shoes are flung off. Padding around shoe-free allows the toes to spread, which is crucial for good balance and for not smudging your nail polish after a perfect pedicure. And the no news bit? Relax your mind by not discussing topical events that can raise your blood pressure sky-high.

- **Adopt time anarchy** Spas are not governed by time. The idea being that you float around in tune to your own circadian rhythms – meaning your internal clock seems to know what to do and when. So move clocks and take watches off.
- **Heat the towels** Put the towels on the radiators so that they're warm when placed on the body after a shower scrub or a massage.
- **Be creative with pillows** I've mentioned pillows before, but to create a spa-style luxury feeling, place them under the knees and feet when lying down and relaxing.
- **Prepare before cleansing** A good facialist will never treat the skin before preparing it. A pampering skin ritual to start off with is to steep a flannel in tepid water with a drop of lavender essential oil, wring it out and place it over the face for a minute or so.
- **Be two faced** Still talking skin, a professional will always adapt your skin products to suit your skin type. Not all skin on the face behaves in the same way, so use a moisturising mask for the cheeks if dry and a clay mask for forehead, chin and nose if they tend to be oily.
- **Milk your beauty** Spas love using milk as it feels wonderfully luxurious on the skin and leaves the body feeling truly nourished.

Try this recipe:

THE CLEOPATRA MILK AND HONEY SMOOTHIE
Have silky skin like Cleopatra, who is said to have bathed in milk for beautiful skin.

You will need
5 tablespoons powdered milk
4 tablespoons clear honey
2 tablespoons sesame oil

Smooth it all over
1 *Mix the powdered milk with enough hot water to create a runny, smooth paste. Mix the honey and sesame oil, and heat gently in a microwave or a small pan until warm.*

2 *Apply the honey and oil mixture to your body using long massage movements. Lie down on a towel for 10 minutes.*

3 *Remove the mixture with the warm milk paste and a flannel. The milk not only helps the honey to glide off but it also moisturises the body something wonderful, too.*

CHAPTER 8

A fabulous makeover

What could be better than including some well-deserved beauty makeovers in one of your girls' nights in? Discovering and trying out new hair and make-up tricks can really spice up your evening in between playing games and having fun. Use this chapter as an insider's guide to creating great new looks where fuller hair, sexier lips and higher cheekbones, along with great body secrets, are all possible by following the beauty step-by-step routines. Professional secrets are revealed, too, so friends can come away from their night boasting new skills! Nothing bonds girlfriends faster than dabbling in beauty can-dos together. It's just one of life's many girlie pleasures and makes any night in (however dressy or casual) so much more fun.

You need a fabulous makeover night in if

- Your look is circa 1992.
- You've been dumped (a never-been-worn lipstick shade or making your lashes look sexier acts as an instant mood lifter).
- You're a frustrated beauty assistant.
- You use your blusher to cover blemishes.
- Your eyebrows resemble a small forest.

A girl's eight biggest beauty lessons

Try these tips for a professional finish to your make-up.

1 HOW TO MAKE YOUR MAKE-UP LAST

You want lipstick left on your lips, not his collar. Make-up that wanders off is annoying. After all, you've put it on to enhance your beauty not to leave your face looking naked and eyes left smudged panda-style halfway through the night. Here's how to make it stay the course.

- **Brush on your base** Your fingertips can leave oil on your face that dissolves make-up within hours. Apply base with a foundation brush. After covering any blemishes with a cream concealer, stroke foundation over the skin with a brush. Don't use a sponge, as they tend to leave streaks of colour rather than a seamless finish. Brush downwards to make any fine hair lie flat on the face. Finish by pressing foundation into the skin with a puff.

- **Prime the eyes** It takes only seconds but has the effect of making shadows last for hours. Smooth the lids with oil-free foundation to keep shadows long lasting and non-creasing.
- **Opt for powder shadows** They last longer than creams, which can literally melt away into the skin. Press on rather than sweep onto the lids. This helps the pigments stick.
- **Double up on blush** This trick really works to keep your blush looking nicely flushed. Swirl an oil-free cream onto the cheeks and then brush a powder blush in a similar shade over it to set the colour. Press a translucent powder into the skin.
- **Line for long-lasting lips** Coat lips with an anti-feathering product. Then with a lipliner that matches your lipstick, draw over the entire mouth to create a non-budge base stain. Stroke on a lipstick with a brush, then cover with one ply of a tissue and pat loose powder through the tissue with a puff. Finally, apply a second layer of lipstick.

Professional make-up secret To banish dark circles under the eyes, dab a small brush into a cream concealer and then swish it around in your palm to warm up the product. This will help it go on smoothly. Sweep the brush from the inner side of your nose all the way to the outer corner of your eye. Pat with your ring finger to blend evenly.

2 HOW TO GET PERFECTLY ARCHED BROWS

Becoming your own brow specialist needs good light, so blow out the candles and turn up the lights. You don't want to end up plucking your brows clean away!

1. Your first step is to plan rather than pluck. A well-shaped brow is universally flattering, so get it right with the help of a pencil. Place a pencil vertically against the nose, covering one nostril. The spot where the pencil meets the forehead is where you brow should begin. To pinpoint the top of the arch, angle the pencil so that it crosses from the centre of the bottom lip

to the iris. For the brow's ending point, angle the pencil from the centre of the bottom lip to the outer corner of the eye. Mark each spot with a brow pencil.

2. Start by tweezing stray hairs between the brows (monobrows went out with the Stone Age) and beneath the brow bones. Trim extra-long hairs by brushing up brows with a brow brush straight up towards the forehead. Trim straight across the ends of any hairs sticking up with a pair of manicure scissors. This is where a girlfriend can step in and help – just make sure she's sober! If you're not completely confident about using scissors, leave it. Cutting too much can create bare patches that can't always be disguised with a brow pencil.

3. Tweeze a clean and even line along the bottom of the brows, switching from one brow to the other every three or four hairs to ensure balance. Tweeze so that brows slant gradually upwards towards the arch, then downwards towards the outer end.

4. Fill in brows with a pencil. Just make sure it's the same shade as your base hair colour.

Professional plucking secret The correct pair of tweezers can make or break a good pluck! Choose tweezers with a slanted edge and a lot of spring. And pull skin taut before plucking to reduce the sting. This also makes it easier to see the line of the brow.

> ### (Very) modern eye looks
>
> Alluring eyes are seemingly the trademark for any stop-'em-in-their-tracks make-up look, so trash your beige eye shadow and look to new looks that seduce. Encourage your girlfriends to turn into make-up artists for the evening by helping to apply eye make-up.

3 HOW TO GET A SEXY, SMOKY EYE

Use gentle strokes to soften liquid eyeshadows for a great look.

1. Use black, silver or brown liquid eyeshadows to achieve a smoky, smudgeable, just-rolled-out-of-satin-sheets vibe.
2. Taking a small brush, smudge mixed shadow onto the lids from the upper lashes to the crease in the socket line. Drag it out beyond the corners of the eyes. Use the same brush to smudge along the base of the lower lashes. You want the effect to look sheer, not dense and heavy. Apply two coats of mascara.

4 HOW TO GET AN ULTRA-MODERN METALLIC EYE

A stunning effect for the eyes; great for clubbing and partying.

1. Line all around the eyes and along the crease with a soft, brown eye pencil.
2. Choosing a metallic chocolate brown eye shadow, apply as a thin line at the base of the upper and lower lashes and along the crease with an eyeshadow brush, then blend out. This will create a sheer, smudgy effect. Brush towards the outside corners of the eyes, swooping up slightly at the ends.
3. Brush a gold shadow all over the lids from the lashes to the crease. The idea is that you want your lids to glow, as though they've been gold leafed. Apply two coats of black mascara.

5 HOW TO GET A ROCK 'N' KOHL SEX-KITTEN EYE

Try this for a sexy as well as sophisticated look.

1. Using a precision liquid liner, trace along the upper lashes close to the base and finish with a skinny tick.

2. For the perfect seductress flick, draw diagonally upwards at the outer corner of the eye, in line with the bottom, not the top lid. If black looks too stark, try a chocolate brown or deep purple liner. Apply two coats of black mascara.

Professional blending secret Make eyes look bigger for all three looks by smudging a shimmering power or cream on the inner corners of the eyes and blend with a cotton bud.

6 HOW TO GET HIGHER CHEEKBONES

We all know the beauty trick of smiling and dusting or dabbing blusher onto the apples of your cheeks, but how do you go about grabbing stand-out cheekbones? Can they be cheated? Yes they can – here's how to redefine your contours. Instead of girlie pinks and peaches, warmer colours, such as darker pinks and reddy hues, are best for defining. To highlight cheekbones easily, start colour high up on the 'apple' of the cheek and run into the hollow of the cheeks – think the shape of a croissant. The colour should be distinct but diffused with all harsh lines and edges clearly blended away.

Professional blushing secret Skip the foundation and put blush onto bare skin for a fresh and less formal appeal.

7 HOW TO GET FLUTTERY LASHES

Making your lashes so flirty you're literally beating the guys off with a stick takes a little more than mascara. It's a full-blown beauty mission! First off, you need eyelash curlers, as they are the saviours of straight lashes and essential for doe-eyed appeal. Just make sure the rubber part of the curler is clean and intact. Clamp onto the lashes and squeeze gently along the lash line for a few seconds. Next, mascara. Black mascara works for everyone – unless you're really fair of lashes, and then a dark brown works better for your skin tone. To apply, wedge the brush right into the base of the lashes and move up beyond the tips to lengthen. Wait a second and then apply another coat for extra oomph. Lightly brush the lower lashes if you want more drama, but avoid if you have small eyes or smearing problems. If there are any clumps, simply comb out with a mascara comb. Alternatively, you can use a pin if you're very, very careful. Fake lashes can really juice up eyes, but look for individual ones. Either place in the outer corners of the eye for that come-hither look or place alternately along the lash line.

Professional lash secret Always wipe excess mascara off the wand with a tissue to remove clumps. And to make sparse lashes appear thicker, check out lash plumping basecoats before mascara. A lash tint (available from pharmacies) is also a great DIY beautifier, so get a girl-friend to paint your lashes – they act as a great insurance policy for when you can't be bothered with the mascara.

8 HOW TO GET SEXIER LIPS

Unless you're Angelina Jolie every woman would love a bigger pout. Here's the way to getting a fuller-looking lip minus the collagen injections.

1. Exfoliate your lips with a warm, wet facecloth. This helps get rid of any dull skin and instantly makes lips look fuller and pinker. In fact, it's a good habit to get into daily.
2. Next, slick on lip balm or Vaseline. With a nude-coloured lip pencil, run along the Cupid's bow of your upper lip (the V at the centre of your top lip), making sure you follow the natural lip line. Drawing outside the line in the hope of making

your lips look bigger doesn't work. It just looks like you've put on your lipliner blindfolded.

3. Continue to draw a line along your bottom lip. Start in the middle of the lip and the outline one-third of the way towards the corner of your mouth. Stopping short of the corner of the mouth is key to creating the illusion of a fuller lip. Go any further and you'll make your mouth look smaller. Use a cotton bud to blur the line slightly before you apply a creamy, pinkish–nude lipstick over the lips.

Professional lip-plumping secret Dab a spot of high-lighter on your cupid's bow to create a sexy 3-D effect.

Show Your Lipstick, Reveal Your Personality

Lipstick can be the ultimate in female bonding. Tell another girl you like her shade of lipstick and it can lead to all kinds of conversation and confessions! But did you know the shape of your lipstick can reveal a lot about your personality? It's been called The Lipstick Freud Theory. Get your girlfriends to tip their make-up bags out to reveal the shape of their most-used lipstick. You can then discover their hidden lipstick personality.

Lipstick shape Flat tipped
Personality You are a girl of extremely high moral standards. You need everybody's approval, you are scrupulous in what you do and you take good care of yourself. You are utterly trustworthy and hate confrontation.

Lipstick shape Sharp pointed
Personality You like to be the focus of attention and love life. You are full of inspiration and you are curious, but like to remain a mystery to others. Confident and skilful, you can rub people up the wrong way, but once a friend, you are faithful and a friend for life.

Lipstick shape Rounded shape but with a pointed tip
Personality You are a mix of contradictions. You love to stay at home but also love to go out and be sociable; you are a girl of your word, but tend to exaggerate (much to the annoyance of others) when detailing stories. You are opinionated but hate to be criticised.

Lipstick shape Remains its original shape
Personality You always follow the rules, are shy and self-restrained. You hate being the centre of attention and it takes years to persuade you to wear another shade of lipstick!

Beautiful body secrets

How to get smooth skin with a wonderful glow.

FAKING THE BEST TAN

You've heard it a million times: the only safe tan comes in a bottle. But getting one without telltale streaks or splotches isn't always as easy as it's cracked up to be. That's why for mistake-free coverage your girlfriends can come to the rescue, as they can help you with all those hard-to-reach areas. In fact, it's a great treatment to do the night before a Big Date Night for instance. Read on for the professional know-how on getting a tan that looks like you've just stepped off the beach and doubles up as a reminder of your pampering party all week long.

THE GOOF-PROOF SELF-TANNING SECRETS

1. Preparation is the key to a believable sun-drenched colour. As well as shaving legs, underarm and bikini line, it's important to buff your skin until it glows. So step in the shower with an exfoliator for company (see recipe on page 94). A body scrub removes dead skin cells and gives the tan

a good smooth base to start with. Buff extra well on areas such as elbows, wrists, ankles, hands and feet, which are prone to dryness.

2. Dry thoroughly and then apply body moisturiser to ankles, heels, the tops of the toes, kneecaps and elbows. This keeps these spots from drinking up excess tanner and turning a sickly orange.

3. Wearing latex gloves, pour the tanner into your hands and rub them together so that the product evenly coats each palm. Start applying with long, full strokes, then rub in a circular motion. This spreads the tanner in a more even way over the area. If you're using a spray, hold it 20 cm/8 in away from the skin.

4. Work from your lower body up. First, cover the area between each ankle and knees. When finished, apply what remains on your hands to the tops of your feet, ankles and knees. These areas beg for a lighter coat of self-tan. Do the same with your arms, using leftover tanner on your elbows.

5. Grab a girlfriend and have her help with the top of your back and the shoulders. Many self-tanning applications now come with added colour so that you can actively see where you are putting it.

6. Take off your gloves and work from your wrists downwards onto the backs of your hands. Go lighter on your fingers so that the self-tanner

doesn't gather on the knuckles.
7. Wash hands with soap and water.
8. For the face, use a formula specifically for that area, as it's normally lighter in colour and texture. Apply primarily to spots the sun naturally hits when out and about, namely the nose, cheeks and the midpoints of the chin and forehead. Then blend into the hairline using light, wispy movements.

Professional faking-it secret For I-can't-guess-it's-not-real colour, use a make-up sponge instead of your fingers to apply around harder-to-blend spots such as between the toes and fingers, and the elbows.

THE SUPER-SMOOTH BODY SCRUB
Mix 4 cups olive oil to ½ cup brown sugar. Dip in a clean cloth and rub over damp skin.

SELF-TAN BLUNDERS

- Applying (drunk) and in a hurry. Take your time and benefit from a luxury colour.
- Getting dressed too soon. Rushing around and sweating can cause streaks. Chill out in a robe.
- Applying make-up too soon. It affects the development.

SELF-TAN WONDERS

- It makes you look 2.25 kg/5 lb lighter.
- It hides the signs of a hangover.
- It makes you look like you can afford a swanky holiday.

How to get super-smooth (and hair-free) legs

The idea of hot wax, girlfriends and cocktails is hardly the most comforting thought, but waxing your legs on a night in isn't as scary as you might think, especially if you have a girlfriend to help out. Waxing your legs is the ultimate in leg-wear as hairless legs obviously makes them look more touchable, sexier and are a must for fine-denier tights or stockings (hair poking through nylon is not a good look!). Just make sure you have 1cm/½ in of hair (about six week's growth) to work with. Regular waxing also makes hair grow lighter over time, so you need to do it less. Here's how to walk through it:

1. Select your wax of choice. Read the instructions, not just once but twice.
2. Heat the wax in a microwave for the suggested time.

3. Now, this is crucial unless you want to end up in casualty: test the temperature before you start slathering it on. It should feel comfortably warm on the skin – not scorching.

4. Check legs are dry – this is very important.

5. For wax virgins, apply a thin layer of wax to a small area of the leg following the hair-growth direction.

6. Press the muslin strip onto the leg.

7. At the bottom of the strip – the bit closest to your foot – turn a small area back against the strip. It should be resting flat against the strip about to be removed.

8. Lift the end as instructed and quickly pull back towards you. Do not pull up.

9. Grit your teeth gently. The pain will ease in a second or two. Promise!

10. Repeat if you have missed any hairs.

11. Continue until the leg is hair-free.

Professional hot-wax secret It may be worth doing a wax after 'having a meditation moment' as described in Chapter 6, as the best way to prevent the pain of waxing is trying to relax! Also, according to experts, when the client is tense the follicle closes and the wax doesn't reach the root of the hair so the treatment won't be as effective.

The best can-do hair secrets

Get great hair with a salon finish.

> ## The all-you-need tool box for sleek hair
>
> hairdryer obviously!
>
> serum
>
> straightening balm
>
> large bristle paddle brush
>
> ceramic smooth-out straightening irons
>
> hair-shine spray

THE SUPER-SLEEK BLOW-DRY

Don't be fooled that heavenly hair can only be achieved at the salon. Although it may seem you need octopus arms to achieve the perfect blow-dry, with a little salon savvy you can get the same results at home. And if you rope in the help of a girlfriend, that's even better, as the results will look more professional. Like putting on make-up, blow-drying gets easier with practise. And what a kick you get when you finally master how to turn wash-and-wear-go-no-where hair into a highly polished coiffure. Here's the hold-your-hand guide to the mystery that can be the professional blow-dry.

1. Wash the hair and blot with a towel. This rids the hair of excess moisture and speeds up drying time with minimum trauma to the hair.
2. If you don't arm yourself with a decent dryer you're wasting your time. You need one with at least 1,700 watts of power and a variety of heat and speed settings for ultimate flexibility. Also attach a nozzle to the dryer to direct the flow of air. It's amazing how many people don't bother and then wonder why their hair ends up a frizzed-out flop!
3. Apply a few drops of anti-frizz serum or a straightening lotion between your palms and smooth over the hair from the roots to tips. Work it evenly through the hair with your fingers.
4. Rough-dry hair at the roots until it's at least 70 per cent dry. No amount of heat styling is going to make any impact on wet hair. All you're doing is knocking the body out of it.
5. Now comes the bit that makes or breaks your style – you can rope in a friend at this point if you want to. Beginning at the back of the head, use clips to divide the hair into manageable 5 cm/2 in sections. Using a paddle brush, dry each section in a downward motion alongside the

brush to ensure the hair stays straight at all times. To finish each section, give the hair a blast of cold air to set it. Work your way around the head. Other hot-head advice includes holding the nozzle close to the brush to create tension. And take it slow. Move slowly down the length of the hair for maximum results.

6. Next, heat some ceramic straightening irons and run them section by section from the roots to the ends of the hair. This will seal the cuticles of the hair, leaving it almost impossible for any moisture to penetrate the shaft.

7. Let the hair cool then finish with a spritz of glossing spray or run styling cream through the ends.

Professional style secret Always use a clean hairbrush. Not one that is clogged up with product and hair.

The all-you-need tool box for hair with volume

volumising lotion

a round brush perfect for creating or controlling waves

Velcro rollers for hair lift-off

microfine hairspray so only you know what's holding
  your hair!

THE SALON-PERFECT BLOW-DRY WITH VOLUME

1. After washing and conditioning the hair, spray over with a volumising product to ensure lots of gorgeous body.
2. To dry, use a large, round bristle brush to create a smooth look with more volume. Depending on your hair length, it should be 2.5-4 cm/1-1½ in round for shorter hair and 5-7.5 cm/2-3 in for longer hair.
3. Section off the hair as for super-sleek hair, but wrap the hair firmly around the bristle brush. Hold the hair on the brush for a few seconds and hold the nozzle of the dryer slightly underneath the brush to 'lift' the hair.
4. To set in volume, wrap hair around a self-fixing roller. Roll, leave and spray over a light mist of hairspray. This creates a soft fullness that lifts the hair away from the head.
5. Remove the rollers section by section and gently run your fingers through the hair. Fingertip-play with the hair until it starts taking shape. For this style lay off the brush, as dragging bristles through the hair can ruin the shape. Finally, lightly spritz with finishing spray.

Professional style secret When you have finished styling your hair, maintain a firm hands-off policy. Too much handling will make your hair droop.

HOW TO TRIM YOUR FRINGE

Warning! Cutting your own hair isn't usually advised, but there's no harm in a friend trimming up a fringe – just make sure she's sober and uses proper scissors (not kitchen scissors).

- **Start with dry hair** Hair always looks longer when wet and looks a lot shorter when dry.
- **Go natural** Cut your fringe when it's minus any product.
- **Scissor smart** Use only hairdressing scissors (buy them from a chemist). And remember: the smaller the scissors, the more control you will have.
- **Don't go blunt** A blunt fringe is impossible for a non-hairstylist to do accurately and should be left to the professionals. Instead, vertically cut into the fringe until it falls just over the eyebrows. This gives a sexy lived-in fringe.
- **Be skilful** Don't lift the fringe when you cut it; leave it flat to the forehead. And don't create tension by pulling it. Do either and you'll get a shorter fringe than you expected.

- **Take your time** Cut a little at a time. You can always snip more off, but you can never put more back on!

PARTY POOPER Leaving your hostess empty of shampoo/conditioner/mousse and other styling lotions and potions.

PARTY SOOTHER Bringing your own!

HOW TO GET CATWALK HAIR

It's always fun to play around with your hair and create lots of different styles. A model has a posse of stylists at her beck and call backstage at the fashion shows to make her hair look runwayworthy, so a friend's extra pair of hands will always come in handy (excuse the pun) for your night in. Play hairstylist for a night and try out new things on each other. Be inspired to turn heads with these six very different styles to suit all hair lengths and textures along with the all-important hair know-how.

The look: Bad hair meets rock chick

Suits All hair types
The know-how The perfect style for when you're actually having a bad hair day. Apply a strong mousse and blow-

dry hair upside down to give it edgy definition. Work a shine enhancer through individual sections and finish with a light mist of fixing spray.

The look: Hitchcock heroine. Think Grace Kelly in 'High Society'

Suits Long hair, all types

The know-how Best done on hair that's been washed the day before, otherwise it's too slippery to work with. Comb into a sleek side parting and then draw into a mid-height ponytail using a bungee band (fabric-covered elastic) – an elastic band is cruel to the hair. Backcomb the hair in the ponytail to provide lots of body and then smooth with a bristle brush. Secure a thin hair net over the bouffant pony and twist to form sculptural shapes. The hairnet may sound old fashioned, but it's crucial to the look, as it allows you to achieve sharpness and cleanness. Finish with a spritz of hairspray and gloss for a glassy shine.

The look: A sexy side order

Suits All hair types

The know-how Sometimes a change of parting can really update your look. Towel dry hair and form a low side parting from the crown diagonally down towards either temple. Apply a blow-dry lotion or spray gel and blow-dry the hair straight using a flat brush. This keeps the hair around the parting flat to the head. Blow-dry the rest of the hair, pointing the nozzle of the dryer downwards to ensure a high shine. You can cheat and use a hair slide to keep the hair close to the head over the exposed ear. Finish with a light wax or serum for ultimate hold and shine.

The look: Free-spirited gypsy

Suits Long hair, all types

The know-how Spray the hair with a setting spray and separate the hair into big sections. Wrap into coils around large heated tongs. Separate loosely with fingers. The bigger the curls the foxier the look, so, for extra body, set the hair beforehand in five or six large heated rollers and spray with hairspray for extra support. To finish, catch the hair with grips to form pretty, wavy shapes for the ultimate in bohemian style.

The look: High-class pony

Suits Shoulder-length hair and longer

The know-how Forget the schoolyard pony, this pony should look chic. Turn your head upside down and spray all over the hair with an extra-strength fixing spray. Using a large brush, scrape all of the hair into a ponytail at the top of the head. Using straighteners, take sections of the tail, spray with a heat-protecting spray and run the straighteners from top to bottom. Hold the straighteners for a couple of seconds at the end of each section to give a sharp edge. Do the same for each section to complete the pony. To finish, use a gel or cream to define the ends and spray with hairspray for hold.

The look: Rockabilly rock 'n' roll

Suits Those with long fringes

The know-how This look has a great retro feel to it while being very modern. Blow-dry the hair using a mousse to make it easier to work with. Take a slightly off-centre triangular section from the front of the hair and backcomb it until it stands up by itself. Next, mould the hair into a quiff and pin into place. Use a strong-hold hair spray to ensure your quiff stays stiff!

PARTY POOPER Hair that doesn't move. It's so unsexy.

PARTY SOOTHER If wearing hair up, spray a toothbrush with ultra-fine hairspray to smooth down any straggly bits. Just don't use it on your teeth afterwards!

Salon secrets to take to your bathroom

- Choose a gentle shampoo followed with a conditioner to restore the pH balance to your scalp.
- After conditioning, apply cold water to your scalp and massage using a kneading action until a warm glow is felt. This helps increase the flow of blood to the hair follicles and encourages Rapunzel-like hair growth.
- Remember: hair is vulnerable when wet. Brushed hard it can stretch and break. When detangling, do not even think about using a brush. Take a wide-toothed comb and work in sections, starting at the ends, then the middle and, finally, the root.
- When styling choose brushes with pliable bristles and rounded ends to avoid scratching the scalp.
- Also for styling, choose brushes with smooth, nylon bristles, as they glide through the hair, are better for styling and are easier to clean.
- When brushing use gentle but firm pressure. Going heavy-handed causes stress to the scalp and can lead to an overproduction of sebum, which makes hair greasy.
- Avoid sticky waxing products that promise shine. They tend to coat the hair and attract dust. Serums and balms are often cleaner and can also disguise split ends.

CHAPTER 9

Post night-in post-mortem

This is a mini chapter, but I've included it simply because I always think one of the nicest things about throwing a night in is the post-mortem afterwards: who said/confessed/did what, how many bottles of vodka were drunk and who blubbed/laughed and attempted more drunk-dialling than anyone else. Even the smallest of nights in can generate good gossip! The gossip is sometimes even worthy of a night in itself!

And hey, if your night in was such a success, bear in mind that some people make a living out of being a party planner. You never know, it could be a whole new vocation for you if your bash went off with a sizzle and a bang!

Signs you're a party planner in the making

- All the girls you invited came (even if it was only two). If they were going to stay in and wash their hair before you invited them round, then they were able to do this (along with being teased and styled) round at your place.
- The police were called (complaints from neighbours of noise pollution). They left with canapés and a couple of phone numbers.
- You had two gatecrashers. Both I can't-believe-it-gorgeous guys. You explained it was a girls' night.
- You fall into bed with new laughter lines and one big hangover – either brought on from alcohol or life itself.
- You suddenly have a rash of I want-to-be-your-girlfriend calls from girls who have heard your nights in rock.

But with night-in highs come night-in lows. One minute it's all just fancy cocktails, lots of great food and outrageous games, the next it's sitting on a crowded bus going to work and having nothing but Tuesday's episode of *EastEnders* to look forward to. The post night-in blues have landed where your

flying-high-as-a-kite mood is melting quicker than ice out of the freezer. Here's how to handle them:

BEATING THE POST NIGHT-IN BLUES

- Post a cute postcard to each of your girlie guests declaring how much you enjoyed seeing them at your party. It keeps the feelgood feeling going!
- Make use of the leftovers (if there are any) by inviting one or two best-of-your-best friends round to pick over the party.
- Wall-mount the Polaroids taken during the party. Every time you look at them they will make you smile.
- Organise another UGNI. There are plenty of suggestions in this book that can keep your night in forever changing and exciting all year!

INDEX

Note: page numbers in *italics* refer to diagrams.

213